*To*

_____

*From*

_____

*Date*

_____

# OASIS
## OF ELIM

*A 31-Day Devotional*

PASTOR (DR.) JAMES FADEL

# Oasis of Elim

*A 31-Day Devotional*

Copyright © 2018 by Pastor (Dr.) James Fadel

ISBN: 978-0-9895728-7-3

**Published by**

Fadel Publishing International
515 County Road 1118
Greenville, TX 75401
www.jamesofadel.com

**Layout Design by**

Cornerstone Creativity Group LLC
Phone: +1(516) 547-4999
info@thecornerstonepublishers.com
www.thecornerstonepublishers.com

Printed in the United States of America.

# DEDICATION

Dedicated to the goal of a more Spirit-filled and heaven-focused RCCGNA membership.

"Seek ye the LORD while He may found, call upon Him while He Is near. You will seek Me and find Me when you search for Me with all your heart."
(Isaiah 55:6; Jeremiah 29:13)

# ACKNOWLEDGMENTS

I appreciate all my publication team members who invested time and expertise to make this book a reality:

Pastor Gbenga Showunmi of Cornerstone Publishing

Dr. Oluwasayo Ajiboye

Joseph Ayo-Vaughn

Samuel Agbem, Kafanchan, Nigeria

Tioluwani Joshua, Ilorin, Nigeria

Olajumoke Lawal

Dr. Manita Fadel

May the Almighty God bless you more and more!

# CONTENTS

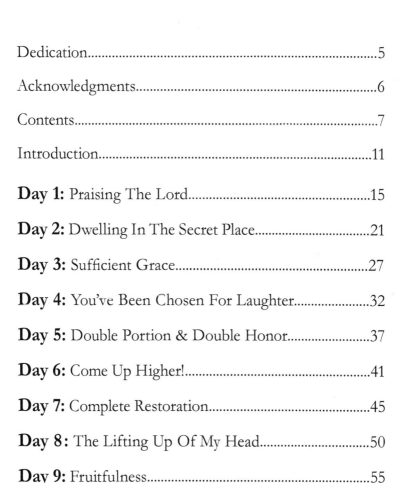

# INTRODUCTION

These daily readings were selected from my monthly
messages to every pastor in The Redeemed Christian
Church of God, North America directory for two and
one-half years. Registered members of The Praying Army
have also received these messages worldwide for two years.
Believers have been blessed, and encouraged, through the
inspired writings, to enter into God's presence regularly.
I felt led to make it available to all as a devotional digest.

> *"And they came to Elim, where were twelve wells of water,
> and threescore and ten palm trees: and they encamped there by
> the waters" (Exodus 15:27).*

After the Hebrews left Marah, they came to the place of
rest and refreshing. They arrived at the Oasis of Elim
where there was an abundance of cool shade and fresh
water to drink. This devotional was assembled as a tool
God can use to bring you to the Oasis of Elim in your
preparation for the daily, weekly, monthly or yearly grind.
God's plan is to fortify you, strengthen you in the inner

man, so that no matter what the enemy throws at you, you are able to withstand him (Ephesians 6:11-17).

God brought the Hebrews through Marah to show them that He Is their Provider in all circumstances, good and bad. We will all come to bitter waters in our life, but it is in those times that we must look to the Tree that God has shown us, the Cross of Christ. Then, it can make those bitter waters sweet, and eventually bring us to Elim. As wonderful and pleasant as Elim was, it was not the intended final destination for the children of Israel. The time came for them to leave. And would you believe that they went back into the wilderness from there (Exodus 16:1a)? To be in a place of peace and prosperity is an awesome thing, but we should never expect to stay there indefinitely.

We are called to be soldiers for the LORD (2 Timothy 2:3-4). As such, though a soldier enjoys rest and recuperation behind friendly lines occasionally, his business is on the battlefield. Therefore, he can be certain that it is there he shall again return. The only reason that the LORD does not snatch us up to Heaven the moment we accept Christ is so that we might fulfill His calling in our lives. As soldiers of the Cross, we are to get His Word out to others, share the Gospel Message with the lost and dying world.

A lot of Christians are basking in the Oasis of Elim, enjoying the peace and prosperity of the Oasis so much that they are unwilling to go back out into the Wilderness. They somehow believe that God's ultimate purpose for them is to live in luxury and soak up the comforts of this world. But if we are to stay in the will of God, we must be ready to follow the "Pillar" when It moves. We must go wherever the Holy Spirit is leading, if we are to make it ultimately to the land that flows with milk and honey (Exodus 3:8; Revelation 21:22-25; Revelation 22:4-5). Nothing should make us stop short of the ultimate that God has predetermined is ours even before the foundations of the earth were laid.

To God goes all glory when we are all He has designed us to be in service to Him.

**Pastor (Dr.) James O. Fadel**
Dallas, Texas
May 2018

# DAY 1

# PRAISING THE LORD

*"It is a good thing to give thanks unto the LORD, and to sing praises unto Thy name, O Most High" (Psalms 92:1)*

Today, we want to praise the LORD, celebrate Him, eulogize Him, honor Him, extol Him, and appreciate Him. He Is the mighty God, awesome, powerful, all-loving, all-gracious, almighty God. The wonder working God that does wonders. Exodus 15:11 says, "Who is like unto Thee, O LORD, among the gods? Who is like Thee, glorious in holiness, fearful in praises, doing wonders?" Praise Him for yesterday, today, and the many days yet to come. Praise Him forever!

Psalms 92:1 says, "It is a good thing to give thanks unto the LORD, and to sing praises unto Thy name, O Most High" There are many good things God expects from His children, e.g. to laugh more, dance more, date your wife more, win more souls, pray more, fast more etc. However, one thing you can do even better is to thank and praise Him more!

# The question is; why must I praise the LORD today?

1. Praising the LORD is a good thing. 1 Peter 3:13 says, "...and who is he that will harm you, if ye be followers of that which is good?" It is a good thing to praise the LORD because it pleases the LORD.

2. Praising the LORD gives you access to His Presence. Psalms 100:4 says to *"Enter into His gates with thanksgiving, and into His courts with praise: be thankful unto Him, and bless His Name."*

3. By praising God, we are doing for God what He cannot do for Himself. God wants His children to praise Him voluntarily, not by compulsion. Psalms 139:14 declares this: *"...I will praise Thee; for I am fearfully and wonderfully made: marvelous are Thy works; and that my soul knoweth right well."* Psalms 67:3,5 declares also to *"Let the people praise Thee, O LORD...let all the people praise Thee."*

4. 4. Praising the LORD demonstrates an attitude of gratitude.

5. Praising Him shows that we're not forgetful of all of His benefits, mercies, forgiveness, healings, victories, touch, and anointing. Psalms 103:1-5 says, *"...Bless the LORD, O my soul and forget not all His benefits".*

6. Praising the LORD helps conquer the pride of self-achievement. It shows you acknowledge that if not for God, you'll be less than zero. James 1:17 tells us that "Every good gift and every perfect gift is from above, and cometh down from the Father of lights, with whom is no variableness, neither shadow of turning."

16

7. Praising the LORD shows the certainty of knowing that God is our source. Psalms 127:1 says, *"Except the LORD build the house, they labor in vain that build it: except the LORD keep the city, the watchman waketh but in vain."*

8. Praising the LORD demonstrates our understanding that our future is in His Hands. He is doing something in and with your life now. He has done somethings in the past and will still do more by His grace. 1 Thessalonians 5:18 admonishes us thus: *"In everything give thanks: for this is the will of God in Christ Jesus concerning you."*

9. Anything you praise the LORD for, you'll never weep over again. John 11:35 says, "Jesus wept." However, in John 11:41, Jesus said, "...Father I thank Thee for Thou hast heard Me." After thanking and praising the Father, Lazarus came forth in verse 43.

10. Anything you praise God for will forever be 'whole'. Luke 17:16-19 says, *"...only one leper came back with a loud voice and glorified God: ...thy faith has made thee whole"*.

## How do I praise God throughout today?

• Praise Him joyfully. "Strengthened with all might, according to His glorious power, unto all patience and long- suffering with joyfulness..." (Colossians 1:11-14).

• Praise Him loudly. "And one of them, when he saw that he was healed, turned back, and with a loud voice glorified God" (Luke 17:15).

• Praise Him with a dance. "... and David danced before the LORD with all his might; and David was girded with a linen ephod" (2 Samuel 6:13-14).

- Praise Him substantially. "And Solomon went up thither to the brazen altar before the LORD, which was at the tabernacle of the congregation, and offered a thousand burnt offerings upon ..." (2 Chronicles 1:6-7).

- Praise Him sacrificially. "And let them sacrifice the sacrifices of thanksgiving, and declare His works with rejoicing" (Psalms 107:22).

- Praise Him to overflowing. "...rooted and built up in Him, and established in the faith, as ye have been taught, abounding therein with thanksgiving" (Colossians 2:6-7).

- Praise Him continually. "By Him therefore let us offer the sacrifice of praise to God continually, that is, the fruit of our lips, giving thanks to His Name" (Hebrews 13:15).

## PRAISE POINTS

1. I praise You, O LORD, because you are God and not a man (Numbers 23:19).

2. I praise You, O LORD, for the salvation of my soul; that God has not given me up to a reprobate mind (Romans 1:28).

3. Thank You for the power to become Your son (John 1:12).

4. Thank You for making all grace abound towards me... always having all sufficiency in all things (2 Corinthians 9:8).

5. I praise, You LORD, because You're working, shining and healing through me.

6. Thank You, LORD, for waking me up, speeding me up, and moving me up, etc.

7. Thank You, LORD; no more losses. Hallelujah!

Now that you know why you should just praise the LORD, happy and blessed are you as you do so!

## DAY 2

# DWELLING IN THE SECRET PLACE

*"He that dwelleth in the Secret Place of the Most High shall abide under the shadow of the Almighty" (Psalms 91:1).*

The LORD wants us to dwell in His Secret Place! Psalms 91 is about God's refuge, protection, security and safety - wherever the beneficiary may be located. It is an amazing psalm filled with hope and lots of promises. Even Satan knows the psalms and he memorized it, deviously quoting it during the temptation of Christ in Matthew 4.

To understand the phrase, "He that dwells in the Secret Place of the Most High," one must look at its composite parts. In Hebrew, the word for "Most High" is the word *"El-yon."* It means "the Supreme One," "the Owner of heaven and earth," and "the God Who Is over and above all things that are." The Secret Place of the Most High gives us a hint of where God wants every believer to be.

To understand what this means is to be a long way toward the fire and purity of revival.

The LORD Jesus Himself came to reveal to us the mystery of the Secret Place and unlock the door. He says, "Abide in Me, and I will abide in you" (John 15:4). Anyone that reads Psalms 91 and reads John 15 along with it will immediately see a striking similarity. The language is the same. The key words in the two passages, abide, dwell, live, mean the same thing.

*"He who dwells in the Secret Place of the Most High shall abide under the shadow of the Almighty" goes right together with "Abide in Me, and I will abide in you".*

That Secret Place is one of physical safety and security, however, access to it is conditional. The Secret Place is a call to the most intense experience that a person can have, the Secret Place is the very essence of personal relationship.

Humans have no inbuilt shelter. Alone, they stand empty and unprotected against the elements; they must run to the Ultimate Shelter Himself. In Psalms 91:1, God offers us more than protection; it is as if He rolls out the hospitality mat and He Is personally inviting us to come in. He lists the conditions we must meet before mentioning the promises that are included in His offer. He wants us to do our part. He wants us to choose to dwell in the shelter of the Most High – first; then, and only then, will we abide under the shadows of the Almighty.

## SIGNIFICANCES OF THE SECRET PLACE

The Secret Place is secret! It is not known to everyone. It

is not liked by everyone. The Secret Place is hard to find, and/ or it could simply be difficult to get to. But for the individuals that desire to get to The Secret Place, hardship or difficulties are immaterial. Since this Secret Place is somewhere that is close to the Most High, the Almighty, it is a really dangerous place to be! When God met Moses on the mountain, He told him that he could not look on His face as it would mean death. He put Moses in the cleft of the rock and placed His hand over him as He walked by. Even this fleeting glimpse of the Ancient of Days caused Moses to glow with the glory of God. To be in The Secret Place is to be pure in heart and clean of hands as Psalms 24 demands. No sin can dwell there. Those that dwell there will glow with the glory of God!

The second significance is that we are to "dwell there!" We must "live there," take up residence there; it must become our address. God invites us to pack up and move to His secret place. If the face of Moses, who only had a brief time on the mountain with God, glowed with His glory, what glory it will be for us to live next to the Almighty. How much will we glow when we live right in His Presence?! Our permanent abode ought to be God's Secret Place.

This is not a call to abandon your wife and children, as our God values relationships! Rather, you are to do your best to bring them along with you, as the head of the home, to the Secret Place (Joshua 24:15).

The person who dwells in the Secret Place must walk away from the clamor. He or she must turn away from the enticements of the world. He or she must be willing to quiet his or her heart before Him. The person must allow

Him to investigate those inner secrets that he or she reveals to no one else (Psalms 139:23-24, 19:12-14). The Secret Place demands honesty and trust. No one can join God in His Secret Place unless he or she is willing to be transparent and honest.

## BLESSINGS OF THE SECRET PLACE

When we choose to leave behind the world's delights in favor of a lifestyle of continual spiritual contemplation, God draws near to us in new ways (James 4:8). We begin to see our sins the way He sees them (Isaiah 6:1–5). The time spent in the presence of God reveals our true thoughts and selfish motivations that might otherwise go unnoticed. In the Secret Place, the fruit of the Spirit takes root and grows (Galatians 5:22-24). We begin to see our lives from an eternal perspective. Earthly frustrations lose significance. We begin to enjoy the LORD's stored up goodness in the Secret Place (Psalms 31:19-20). He will break all obstacles in our way. God gives to us the treasures of darkness and the wealth of the Secret Places (Isaiah 45:3). All the resources that God has for us are inside this place. We can access all the riches in Christ; we can access all God has for us there. It is a place where I want to be!

The key to moving into the Secret Place is total surrender to the Holy Spirit, and to God's will for our lives. This decision consequently dominates our actions and changes our outlook. As we obey, God meets us in His Secret Place (John 14:21). He teaches us and encourages us to remain inside His dwelling place. If our lives must bear lasting fruit, the power to bear that fruit comes from time spent with the LORD. We must choose to surrender fully to

Him in the Secret Place (John 15:4–5; 1 Corinthians 3:14–15; Psalms 92:12–14).

The Holy Spirit came not just to quicken and save us (John 6:44-45; 1 Corinthians 1:18,21); He desires to have intimate relations with us and be the source of the fire and zeal within us (2 Corinthians 13:14; John 14:23,26, 15:13-15). Oh, that we would cling to Him and seek Him in the Secret Place. Oh, that we would seek His fire, His fullness and His Presence. We must seek Him for His love and Presence alone. We must seek Him in humility and brokenness. We will not be disappointed if we seek Him. We must let revival start with us.

## PRAYERS

1. Bless His Majesty, praise His Holy Name – Jehovah Shalom, Jehovah Elohim, All Knowing, All Powerful, All Sufficient, The Monarch of the Universe, Ancient of Days, Rock of Ages, etc. Worship Him!

2. As the hart panteth after the water brooks, so panteth my soul after thee, O God. My soul thirsteth for God, for the living God: when shall I come and appear before God? (Psalms 42:1-2)

3. Holy Spirit, please sustain me in the place of closeness to You so that I may continue to enjoy the bounty of heaven.

4. LORD Jesus, please shield me from every power that causes a leak of Your blessings from my life, in Jesus' Name.

5. Father, please send Your fire to destroy every altar

erected against my ability to continue to preach the Good News, in Jesus' Name (Acts 23:12).

6. LORD, as I dwell in Your Secret Place, I pray that no unbeliever around me will outshine me, in Jesus' Name. I shall be found to be better than the best of them around me, in Jesus' Name (Daniel 1:19-20).

7. Father, as I dwell in Your Secret Place, let my ears be opened to the voice of Your Spirit, in Jesus' Name (Revelations 2:29).

8. Holy Spirit, please shield my eyes away from things that will misinform my heart, in Jesus' Name (2 Samuel 12:21-23)!

9. Thank You, Holy Spirit, for prayers answered, in Jesus' Name!

# DAY 3

# SUFFICIENT GRACE

*"... And He said unto me, 'My grace is sufficient for thee: for My strength is made perfect in weakness.' Most gladly therefore will I rather glory in my infirmities, that the power of Christ may rest upon me" (2 Corinthians 12:9).*

We bless God for the victories, breakthroughs, battles fought and won in the past few days and those of the days to come. Today, God wants us to focus on 'Sufficient Grace'; the grace that enables one to operate in one's God-given capacity to the fullest (Ephesians 4:7; 2 Corinthians 12:9).

If Christ tarries, we shall deal with other kinds of graces later, such as: Abundant Grace, Saving Grace, Great Grace, Exceeding Grace, Manifold Grace and Amazing Grace. Winning in life goes beyond human strength, smartness, tireless input, and wisdom alone. Undoubtedly, these are skills required for progress and greatness. However, on their own, they are grossly insufficient to give you the kind of progress that God has ordained for you. No wonder David said in Psalms 127:1, "Except the LORD build the house...." Behind the making of any man in God's kingdom is the "GRACE OF GOD" (1 Corinthians 1:26-29). So, what looks like a handicap or limitation in your life might be the reason God has called you. He wants to make nonsense of the wisdom of the world. If you do not appreciate the place of grace as you go higher in life, you may end up in DISGRACE.

Salvation, sanctification, and the hope of Heaven are all the handiwork of Grace. A long time ago, some religious experts were debating on what sets Christianity apart from other philosophies, theories and religions. C.S. Lewis simply said, "It's Grace".

La Juan Morris said:

> *"Grace is our source of power when problems are perplexing. Grace is the spring of our tenacity when trials trip us up. Grace is the element of hope when we feel harassed and helpless. Grace is the frontier of our faith during frustration. Grace allows us in times of trouble to look up instead of falling out."*

Do you want to exceed your size, or operate beyond the realms of human wisdom, skill and intelligence? You need grace the size of God to become unstoppable. The LORD wants us to focus on sufficient grace today because God's sufficient grace is needed:

1.  **For endurance**: It will take you through any kind of physical, spiritual and emotional pain, no matter how long that pain exists. This grace will sustain you until when HE determines the pain should go. (2 Corinthians 12:9).

2. **To empower us to flourish and succeed:** Until Grace came, the mountain that withstood Zerubbabel did not become plain (Zechariah 4:6-7).

3. **To serve the LORD:** Moses stammered and wanted to use that as an excuse not to work for God, but God gave him the grace needed to work for Him (Exodus 4:10-11).

4. **When you're facing storms and doubts:** Peter 's faith shook when he saw the storm (Mark 14:30-31). The needed grace to overcome every storm of life, was received in Jesus' Name.

5. **Because hopelessness and depression can cripple even the strongest Christian (1 Kings 19:3-8):** Elijah complained to God that he may die because of Jezebel's threat. The LORD came to his aid, and he was restored to his state of anointing.

God does not lift the already lifted. He is looking for the helpless and the lowly who are heavily dependent on Him. The question is, "Do you need Him?" Without God, you can do nothing; you must acknowledge your helplessness before you can be linked with divine, sufficient Grace and power. Do you know that Grace brings favor without labor? Or that Grace makes promotion possible without any qualification attached to it? When Grace speaks:

• Protocols are suspended, as in the case of Esther.

• Laws of the land are broken, as in the case of King David.

• Educational qualifications are unnecessary, as was true for Peter.

- Connections are needless, as Grace connected Joseph to a higher place and he went from being a prisoner to being the prime minister in a foreign land in one day!

Today, I decree that the Grace of God will speak on your behalf in your family, and in every area of your life. It will see you flourishing from race to grace today and forever, in Jesus' Name. Amen.

So, soldiers of the cross, do not despair, His grace is sufficient for all the battles you're facing.

"... *After you have suffered for a little while, the God of all grace, who called you to His eternal glory in Christ, will Himself PERFECT, CONFIRM, STRENGTHEN and ESTABLISH you.*" 1 Peter 5:10 (NASB).

## PRAYERS

1. Father, I Thank You for Your abundant grace, sufficient grace, saving grace, great grace, exceeding grace, manifold grace and amazing grace, in Jesus' Name.

2. God of grace, bestow on me grace commensurate to the assignment You have given me, in Jesus' Name.

3. Father, let Your grace ,which qualifies the unqualified, rain abundantly upon me, in Jesus' Name. Please LORD, give me the grace to live a life that is in alignment with Your will, in Jesus' Name.

4. Heavenly Father, I decree in the Name of Jesus Christ that all forces and powers that may be frustrating the grace of God, in my life, family, ministry, and Your

purpose for my life, be frustrated, in Jesus' Name.

5. God of all Grace, establish Your total counsel and perfect every imperfection in my life, in Jesus' Name.

6. Father, let Your grace and favor catapult me to a place of glory and move me to my next level of greatness, in Jesus' Name.

7. Father of all grace, let Your grace preserve me for Your coming, in Jesus' Name.

# YOU'VE BEEN CHOSEN FOR LAUGHTER

*"Then was our mouths filled with laughter and our tongues with singing; then said they among the heathen; The LORD hath done great things for them" (Psalms 126:2).*

We serve a God who fills the mouths of His chosen with laughter. Some of His chosen testified to this in Psalms 126:2 saying, "Then was our mouths filled with laughter and our tongues with singing; then said they among the heathen; The LORD hath done great things for them." The word of God is His law. God's laws are the highest and most sovereign of all laws. When the word of the LORD comes concerning any situation in a man's life, it suspends all prevailing laws; it revokes, reverses and annuls the operations or terms of reference of any other law; it limits life's limitations and converts life's impossibilities into testimonies of laughter!

Merriam Webster's dictionary describes laughter as "a

cause of merriment; to show emotion such as mirth, joy, or scorn with a chuckle or explosive vocal sound; to find amusement or pleasure in something." The devil has been contending over God's privileges for you, but you can engage him head on. Ephesians 6:12 says, "we wrestle… against principalities, powers, rulers of darkness and spiritual wickedness in high places". We are fighting 'in victory' not 'for victory' because Jesus Christ of Nazareth bruised the head of the devil over two thousand years ago. So, this is your day of laughter!

Next to love, laughter has been described as the second most powerful emotion we can express. It's been said that "laughter is like internal jogging; it stimulates the respiratory system, it oxygenates the body, it relaxes the muscles and opens pleasure-producing channels in the brain." No wonder the Bible said in Proverbs 17:22 that "A merry heart doeth good like medicine, but a broken spirit dries up the bones." You must laugh this day.

Look at examples in the Bible, in Genesis 18:1-14, when the LORD visited Abraham and Sarah, and ate in their tent, He promised them that they would have a son in nine months' time; but Sarah laughed because her husband was over 99 years old and she herself was 90 years old. She thought that this promise was a joke borne out of how much the visitors enjoyed the meal that she prepared. God asked why she laughed, but she denied that she laughed. Nine months later, she gave birth to a son named laughter and she laughed for the rest of her life (Genesis 21:6).

Today, God still makes people laugh. When God makes you laugh, your laughter will be sustained. But how can God make you laugh today? God makes you laugh when you receive a divine visitation. It is one thing for you to visit with God, like in your daily devotional time, but it is another thing for God to visit you. It is a beautiful experience when God visits a congregation, or a group of people, but it is even lovelier when God picks out an individual in a large congregation for divine visitation. The LORD will single you out for a divine visitation this season in Jesus' Name!

In John 5:2-9, there was a multitude of sick folks at Bethesda, but when Jesus visited, he went straight for the man who had been sick for 38 years, healed him and left the place. Similarly, in Mark 10:46-52, Jesus entered Jericho and passed through it looking for whom to visit. He saw no one in Jericho, but as He was leaving, in the midst of a crowd, he saw a blind beggar outside the city gate, healed him, and continued with His journey. As Jesus healed these people, He introduced laughter into their lives. There was no record that either of them was ever sick again. Whatever criteria He uses to determine candidates for His visitation shall work in your favor today.

As you receive God's Word concerning any aspect of, or situation in, your life, and declare it in warfare today, every hopelessness and helplessness will bow; the irreversible will be reversed, the irrevocable will be revoked, and the humanly unimaginable will be delivered to you at no personal cost. I am believing with you this day that out of the crowd of those who need children, the LORD will visit you and yours. Out of the crowd of those who need promotions, the LORD will promote you. Out of the multitude of those who need special anointing, the LORD will visit you especially today, in Jesus' Name. However, make sure to flee from sin, and do only what pleases Him.

Be faithful in the giving of your tithes and offering, and worship Him. Give a special offering to the God of the Praying Army.

## PRAYERS

1. Begin to thank God for today and for helping, strengthening, and empowering you.

2. Thank Him for the rest of this day and for your life; "...you shall tread upon serpents, scorpions and all the power of the enemy—nothing shall by any means hurt you" (Luke 10:19).

3. It is written, "For with God nothing shall be impossible" (Luke 1:37). Therefore, every impossible situation facing me now, turn to a testimony of laughter, in Jesus' Name.

4. Every law in the spirit realm that is imposing impossibility and limitations upon my life and destiny, be revoked and annulled now by fire, in Jesus' Name.

5. Ye doors of miracles, signs and wonders, open wide unto me in all areas of my life from today and for the rest of my life, in Jesus' Name.

6. Father, I have wept for too long. From now on, introduce laughter into my life and make me laugh forever, in Jesus' Name.

7. Father, You caused Sarah to laugh at 90 years old. You made Elizabeth laugh in her old age. You even suspended the prevailing law of science for the virgin, Mary. Please, do mine too, in Jesus' Name!

8. Thank You, LORD, because You'll crown this year with Thy goodness (bountiful harvest), and Your path [for me] will drip with fatness (abundance of joy, celebration and laughter), in Jesus' Name (Psalms 65:11).

## DAY 5

# DOUBLE PORTION & DOUBLE HONOR

*"Turn you to the stronghold, ye prisoners of hope: even today do I declare that I will render double unto thee" (Zechariah 9:12).*

This day shall be your day of a double inheritance, and a double portion of God's Spirit, and double honor, in Jesus' Name. Zechariah 9:12 says, "Turn you to the stronghold, ye prisoners of hope: even today do I declare that I will render double unto thee."

In the Jewish culture, the eldest or the first male child is entitled to an inheritance of a double portion. This day, God is granting this special privilege, and unique blessing, to a selected few, with the added responsibility of being a firstborn. Will you accept these blessings and consequent responsibilities? Throughout the Scriptures, anytime God blesses His people, He adds a responsibility, so they can remain in His blessings and also qualify for the next level of blessing. Here are God's promises for your double portion: Isaiah 45:1; Zechariah 9:12; Exodus 22:7; 1 Timothy 5:17.

Let us look at several examples of men who received the double portion with the prerequisite qualification for the it:

1. **Job:** Job was a man who received the double portion (Job 42:10).

Qualification - He was a leader among many. The LORD said, "There is none like him on the earth, one who fear God and shuns evil" (Job 1:8). He was a man of excellent character.

Not only was Job a good role model for husbands and fathers, he was sensitive to the needs of the oppressed and poor (Job 29:12-17, 31:13-22). Job was morally pure, guarding carefully his eyes and emotions (Job 31:1-12). He was a man of vision with a sense of destiny. This type of life must be reproduced in the lives of men and women who need a double portion.

2. **Elisha:** (2 Kings 2:9). This is another classic example of a man who received the blessings of the double portion.

Qualification - He was not a son who inherited the blessing from a natural father, but from a spiritual father, Elijah. The prophet Elijah had many spiritual sons, but Elisha had several characteristics that promoted him above other sons of the prophet. Elisha was a servant to Elijah. He was industrious, hard-working, steadfast, and loyal. When he is first mentioned in scripture, we find him laboring in the field with twelve yokes of oxen (1 Kings 19:19).

Elisha never allowed boredom or laziness to rule his life.

He was a man of purpose and he valued relationships. Elisha never became arrogant or independent after receiving the good teaching and prophetic mantle from his spiritual father, Elijah. He remained teachable and loyal to his master right up until the time of their parting. Do you want a double portion? Be a man/woman of purpose who values relationships. Oh, by the way, who is your spiritual father?

**3. Joseph**: Although, he was the 11th son, he emerged as the firstborn with the double portion from among all the brethren (Genesis 48:5; 1 Chronicles 5:1-2).

Qualification - Joseph was very righteous and spiritual even as a child (Ezekiel 47:13). His brothers, on the other hand, were evil (Genesis 37:1-11). He overcame discouragement. Joseph had to overcome a bad childhood in a hostile domestic atmosphere; rejection and cruelty of his brethren, exile, slavery, loneliness, homesickness, sexual temptations, false accusations, imprisonment, a ruined reputation, and many other injustices. In addition to all of these, he had to endure long and painful delays, and battle against tremendous doubt and discouragement. Yet every injustice became a tool that moved him closer to the throne. Every delay, heartache, and difficulty was building in him the back bone, character, and will required for the great task he was called to perform. He also developed the great capacity to forgive his brothers. His first son was called Manasseh, meaning 'God has made me to forget' (Genesis 41:51). Can you forget the injustices of yesterday?

If you want a double portion, simply do what Job, Elisha and Joseph did, and you shall receive what they received.

# PRAYERS

1. Thank God for He is the same yesterday, and today and forever (Hebrews. 11:8). Thank Him for not being a respecter of persons (Acts 10:34).

2. Thank Him for this new day of double portion, double honor and double inheritance.

3. Plead the blood of Jesus upon your life for redemption from all sins. Pray that His blood will break every hold and grip of the devil upon your mind, and from now on, your mind shall be yielded and submissive to God's will in Jesus' Name.

4. I dedicate my entire life as a living sacrifice, holy and acceptable to God from today, and for the rest of my life, in Jesus' Name.

5. Father, by your grace and mercy, command double honor, double favor, double promotion, double anointing for me this day, in Jesus' Name.

6. Father, let the Sword of the Spirit do double damage to the camp of my enemies. Let them suffer double destruction today, in Jesus' Name.

7. Father, I receive the Grace to be a man/woman of excellent character like Job; a man/woman of purpose who values relationships like Elisha, and a man/woman who refuses to be discouraged against the odds like Joseph, in Jesus' Name.

8. Begin to thank God for prayers answered.

# DAY 6

# COME UP HIGHER!

*"After these things I looked, and behold, a door standing open in heaven. And the first voice which I heard was like a trumpet speaking with me, saying, "Come up here, and I will show you things which must take place after this" (Revelation 4:1-2).*

Congratulations for the blessing of a new day! I am puzzled about God's direction today. I was thinking God would say it's the day of grace or elevation or something like that. The way God operates is that when He blesses a people, He also gives them a challenge. As they obey, He blesses them even more. This is borne out time and time again in the Scriptures, from Genesis to Revelation. After God blesses His people, He will give them a commandment to keep them in the blessing, so He can bless them even more.

In the text above, there was a call to the Apostle John from the Master to come up higher. God's perpetual invitation to His covenant children is to come up higher! This is an invitation to divine communion, divine companionship, divine fellowship, divine relationship, divine intimacy and initiation. It is an invitation into the reality and experiences of the supernatural. The interesting fact is that in life, you are either going up or coming down. There is no standing still. The moment you stop ascending, you start descending.

The laws of life that hold men and women bound down here are suspended up there.

That is why:

- Isaiah said, "…you will run and never be tired, walk and not faint" (Isaiah 40:31).
- Mary could conceive without meeting with a man.
- Sarah could conceive at the age of ninety years.
- Elijah and Enoch could ascend into heaven and gravity couldn't pull them down.
- Isaac could sow upon a very hard, dry ground in the time of terrible drought and reap a bumper harvest the same year. That is why he was digging wells in the desert and getting water; something that had proven to be an impossibility for the Philistines that were indigenous to the Place.

When Jesus rose up from the dead, "He ascended on high, sitting at God's right hand, principalities and powers being made subject unto him" (Ephesians 1:19-23). He's ruling and reigning there. As God is busy beckoning unto his children to "come up higher", Satan is ferociously, yet deceptively, beckoning "come down." Satan is against anyone going up. He wants men to come down. People with great, colorful destinies that were destined to be the envy of humanity and angels crashed into the abyss of meaninglessness and forgetfulness.

- Adam was created for grandeur, glory and honor. He honored an invitation from the enemy of his soul, and came crashing down. Anytime you act contrary to God's instruction, no matter how minute the instruction is, you're going down the ladder of life.

- Ahithophel, the witty and weighty presidential advisor, crashed beyond redemption (2 Samuel 16:33, 17:23)

- For Judas, it was for the love of money that he lost his place in the apostleship (Luke 22:5).

- For Gehazi, it was covetousness (2 Kings 5:20-27).

- For Samson, it was the love of women and incorrigibility; what a waste for a man anointed from his mother's womb.

How do you know yours? What's that aspect of your life that everybody is rebuking you for? That part of you that everybody is complaining about? That negative aspect of your life that you justify or give explanations for. Only you can identify it and fight it out. Stop it before it stops you!

## QUALIFICATIONS FOR COMING-UP HIGHER

1. **Redemption**: John 3:6 says, "That which is born of the flesh is flesh and that which is born of the spirit is spirit..." 1 John. 3:9 says, "whosoever is born of God... stops sinning."

2. **Sanctification:** It means to be set apart, consecrated

43

to a holy God. To be sanctified means dead to sin (Colossians 3:5-10), dead to self, to be God-centered (Philippians 2:5-7), and renewed in the mind (Romans 12:1-2).

3. **You must pass the test to come higher:** Be God-focused and God-centered.

4. **Be Holy Spirit-filled:** (Luke 4:1; Acts 2:4). You must have an encounter of being filled with the Holy Spirit with the evidence of speaking in tongues.

5. **Fasting & Prayer:** Matthew 4:1-2 says, " then Jesus was led up by the Spirit into the wilderness…He had fasted forty days and forty nights; afterward He was hungry."

## PRAYERS

1. Faithful God, Thank You for the blessings of today. I am settled, in Jesus' Name.

2. Oh God, lift me above the rock that is higher than I as from today, in Jesus Name.

3. Anointing for divine sight, divine hearing and divine empowerment, fall upon me by fire as from today, in Jesus' Name.

4. Grace to live holy and pure unto God for the rest of my life, I receive Oh LORD, in Jesus' Name.

5. Every limiting law of life that my destiny is responding to, be revoked and annulled by fire now, in Jesus' Name.

# DAY 7

# COMPLETE RESTORATION

*"And I will restore to you the years that the locust hath eaten, the cankerworm, and the caterpillar, and the palmerworm, My great army which I sent among you. And ye shall eat in plenty, and be satisfied, and praise the Name of the LORD your God, that hath dealt wondrously with you: and My people shall never be ashamed" (Joel 2:25-26).*

I want to salute and congratulate you. You made it to see another day. Your portion this day, and for the rest of the coming days, is 'Complete Restoration'. Joel 2:25-26 is your portion, in Jesus' Name. This portion of scripture is a missile for the termination of the losses, disappointments, delays, denials and misfortunes of the past years in a man's life. By His Word, you will get back all that has been stolen or taken away from your life, in Jesus' Name. God's Word has the guarantee and secured assurance of restoration for whatever kind of loss a man might have suffered at any time in his life's journey. Hallelujah!

Hear what God says: "the glory of the latter house shall be greater (surpass, more glorious) than the former..." (Haggai 2:6-8). As the LORD of heaven lives, in this new day, the glory you have lost, by the mercy of the LORD, shall be restored. Be expectant. Satan is a thief. He is the agent and sponsor of losses, but most importantly, God is a Restorer (John 10:10).

▪ Nebuchadnezzar lost his glory for 7 years because of pride (Daniel 4:33-35), but by the mercy of God, he was restored. Everything he had lost in 7 years was restored as if he never lost anything to begin with. By the mercy of God, whatsoever you have lost over the years - glory, promotion, honor, health etc., the God of heaven shall restore, in Jesus' Name.

• The sons of the prophets came to Elisha and said the place we used to dwell in is too small for us (2 Kings. 6:1-7). Elisha told them to go ahead and build a new sanctuary. One of them asked that his father in the LORD come with them mandatorily (vs. 3), and eventually Elisha obliged. While at the work site, felling trees to build the sanctuary with an axe head being used by one of the sons of the prophets fell into the water. "...Alas it was borrowed" (vs. 5). Once Elisha ascertained where the axe head had fallen, upon inquiry, he threw in a stick and the axe head floated up to the surface (vs. 6).It is not an offense to want to expand or increase. God wants you to enlarge your coast, but you do not know what you will encounter along the way. I may not know what you were doing that resulted in the sudden loss of your "axe head." However, by the mercy of God, that cutting edge will swim again.

- The cutting edge was lost not because he was out of the will of God; not that he sinned, but because the assignment was big. I do not know what assignment you have embarked upon that now seems intent on swallowing you up. Nevertheless, I do know that, by the mercy of God, you are not alone.

- They cried, "Master, it was borrowed" (vs. 5 paraphrase). What is it that you borrowed that got lost? By the mercy of God, it shall be restored, in Jesus' mighty Name.

- Thank God their prophet went with them. Thank God they cried out for his help. Just as Elisha asked them, "Where did your axe head fall?", the LORD Is asking you today, "Where did you lose your cutting edge? Why are you struggling today? What is it that has been taken away from you?" The grace of God is in the house today for you to recover all that you have lost, in Jesus' Name.

- Did you see what happened? The man of God cut a stick, dropped it into water, the stick sank, and the axe head swam. The Archimedes law of flotation was displaced; what was heavy floated and what was light sank. Wherever your anointing, health, favor, unction, ability to succeed, etc. has been buried, by the mercy of God, it will rise again. It will rise again seven times.

- Every principle that has kept you down (e.g. the law of gravity), there is a higher principle (i.e. the law of aerodynamics) that will take you up, and keep you up. The higher principle is displacing every other principle, in Jesus' Name. One thing they did was cry out. Do

47

not allow what was buried to swallow you. Cry to the Master today, and you will recover all, in Jesus' Name.

The product of restoration is seen in Joel 2:25-27. Give voice to God's Word today. Release the trigger of restoration from God's Word and your entire destiny shall be restored to its original color and glory (Psalms 8:5-6).

## PRAYERS

1. Begin to thank God for this new day. Thank Him for increasing His Strength, power and mercy unto you today.

2. Father, all that I have lost (opportunity, unction, promotion, favor ), let me recover them again, in the Name of Jesus Christ.

3. According to Joel 2:25-26, Oh God, please begin to restore to me the lost years of my life, in Jesus' Name.

4. Power for divine overtaking, divine speed, and divine settlement in all areas of my life, fall upon me this day, in Jesus' Name.

5. Thou my heavens and my ground, begin to release your rain and increase unto me as from today, in Jesus' Name.

6. I receive a restoration of my lost glory and my cutting edge, health, and soundness. Let my hope rise again, O LORD!

7. Thou customized invitation card from Satan into my life, be roasted by fire. Thou demonic embargoes upon any area of my life, be terminated now by fire, in Jesus' Name.

8. Thou purifying fire of the Holy Spirit, pass through me and destroy every messenger of Satan sent to abort my destiny, in Jesus' Name.

9. Power to say No, when I ought to say No, fall on me. Thou nature of God, be planted in my destiny, in Jesus' Name.

10. I prophesy that I will begin to succeed and make progress in life with ease, in Jesus' Name.

Thank Him for prayers answered, in Jesus' Name.

## DAY 8

# THE LIFTING UP OF MY HEAD

*"But thou, O Lord, art a shield for me; my glory, and the lifter up of mine head" (Psalms 3:3).*


I want to welcome you to the day of the lifting up of our heads. The Almighty God said that today, He wants to bless heads – personal heads, heads of governments, ministries, and companies.

The head, according to the Webster dictionary, is literally described as, *"The part of the body containing the five sensory organs: Brain, Eyes, Ears, Nose and the Tongue."* or *"the seat of emotion"* or *"the first in position.""* Also, in Pastor OJ. Kuye's book, *Deliverance of the Head*, he said, *"The head is the physical and spiritual brain box of the whole body."*

Given these perspectives, it is important to note, however, that there are different kinds of heads. Some heads attract favor, while others disfavor. In like manner, some heads have an easy passage or access in life, while others with similar circumstances, education, upbringing, and same locality are stagnated, and their heavens are like brass. A few Biblical examples are: Jacob & Esau (Malachi 1:2-3); the butler & the baker (Genesis 40:1-23); Herodias & John the Baptist (Mark 4:22-28). The good news is that at Calvary, Jesus bruised the head of the serpent (Genesis 3:15; Colossians 2:13-15). Hallelujah!

God alone is the Lifter of heads. Others may try, but it almost always leads to frustration, and even an aggravation of the original situation. He can lift one from the lowest of places to the highest. He can promote from being common to being uncommon, and He can make a complete zero a hero. My prayer for us today is that The Lifter Up of our heads, Jesus Christ of Nazareth, will heal our heads that they may begin to attract mercy, favor, blessings, fortune, anointing, grace, breakthroughs, etc., in Jesus' Name.

However, in Zechariah 1:19-21, we understand that there are powers that will not let go. These are demonic agents among the rank and file of the enemy's workforce who serve in the department of the horn. Without the intervention of the LORD God of Hosts, these demonic agents will not allow heads to be lifted in the spiritual realm, no matter how valiant the efforts to break free. But, today, our heads shall be lifted, and the horns allied and armored against us shall be frayed, silenced, and consumed by the fire of the Holy Ghost, in Jesus' Name.

As your head is lifted today, may you be given a loud voice of recognition for promotion like Daniel, in Jesus' Name. May you move from obscurity to popularity. May you begin to experience a glorious and positive change in every area of your life. May your greatness begin to spring forth until you become very great, like Isaac. Your head will be lifted to realms where you are out of the reach of your enemies. You will begin to sit with princes and honorable men and women (Psalms 26). No man can demote you, when God lifts your head. Biblical examples of people whose heads were lifted, amongst many, are:

- Abraham, the father of faith.

- Joseph, from slavery & prison to Prime Minister in a foreign land, despite his accent.

- Esther, a housemaid that became Queen.

- Mordecai, a gateman who was promoted, by the king, above the highly placed official who sought to execute him.

- David, no one knew the family of Jesse. His father never introduced David to Prophet Samuel, but the Lifter of heads intervened.

- The three Hebrew slave boys became governors in the land of their captors. Are you spiritually dissatisfied with your present position or situation in life? God wants you lifted, but He has conditions for lifting people up:

- You must be holy within and without (Hebrews 12:14; Leviticus 20:26). A righteous man in the wrong place is no different than a sinner in the right place; neither of them can be blessed by God.

- Be generous and give of your time, talents, and resources both within and outside the church (Psalms 50:5; Matthew 25:35-40).

- Pray, with plenty of zeal, power, and the favor of God,

52

to know the mind of God pertaining to His purpose and design for your life. You must connect with your destiny – know it, pursue it, and never give up.

- Be honest. Remove falsehood and deception from your life. Develop your character and integrity; become a person of your word.

- Pray without ceasing, for your adversary, the devil, roams about without rest, seeking whom to devour. You must deal with the scattering horns in the house of Prayer! You cannot offer a ten-cent prayer and expect a $1,000 answer (James 5:16-17).

## PRAYERS

1. Let us begin by thanking God for creating this day, week, and month for our pleasure. Thank Him for helping you thus far in your journey with Him.

2. My Glory and The Lifter Up of my head, arise! Manifest

3. Your power in my life, in the Name of Jesus.

4. Father, You have made my head the spiritual brain box of my existence and my being. I ask that You supernaturally touch my head, and the foundation of my existence, in Jesus' Name.

5. My Father, my Father, lift my head, in the Name of Jesus.

6. Father, give me total healing and complete deliverance from every sickness of the head, in the Name of Jesus.

7. Put your hands on your head and begin to prophesy over your head: my head is programmed for success

53

and not failure, my head shall respond to good opportunities, promotion, and favor, in the Name of Jesus.

8. Begin to thank God for prayers answered.

# DAY 9

# FRUITFULNESS

*"And he removed from thence, and digged another well; and for that they strove not: and he called the name of it Rehoboth; and he said, For now the Lord hath made room for us, and we shall be fruitful in the land" (Genesis 26:22).*

Blessed be the Name of the LORD, Who has kept us alive to see a new day today. The LORD spoke to Isaac to stay in Gerar and made him fruitful in spite of the famine in the land (Genesis 26:2,6,12-13).

The same God is now congratulating you this day for fruitfulness and He's saying to you "REHOBOTH". That is, the LORD has made room for you, and you shall be fruitful in the land, in Jesus' Name (Genesis 26:22). The Covenant of Fruitfulness shall manifest in your life, in Jesus' Name.

All through the Old Testament, God covenanted fruitfulness with His people; at creation (Genesis 1:26-28), with Noah (Genesis 6:18, 9:1), and with Abraham (Genesis 12:1-3,

17:6). All are covenants of fruitfulness. Initially, Abram (Abraham) stayed at his parent's house before God called him (Genesis 12:1-3). However, since "the end of a matter is greater than the beginning thereof" (Ecclesiastes 7:8), by the time we read of Abram in Genesis 13:2, "...he was very rich in livestock, in silver and in gold." In Genesis 18:14, he was fruitful again and gave birth to Isaac (Laughter). He (God) did it for Abraham even at an old age; He will do yours too, in Jesus' Name.

Likewise, He made Isaac fruitful (Genesis 26:12-14). "Then Isaac sowed in that land, and received in the same year..." Isaac had wanted to leave, resign, and quit because of the famine. He said, "Enough is enough; I will leave the Promised Land." God said, "Don't go; stay where you are, and I will bless you." Then in v. 12, "Isaac sowed in that land, and received in the same year a hundredfold; and the LORD blessed him...and the Philistines envied him". You too will sow and reap a hundred-fold this month, in Jesus' Name.

In keeping to His covenant, God extended the blessing of fruitfulness to yet another descendant of Abraham, Jacob (Israel). Like his predecessors, Jacob also abounded with great wealth. The biblical record tells us that "he increased exceedingly, and had much cattle, and maidservants, and menservants, and camels and asses" (Genesis 30:43).

Jesus, through His life and death on the cross of Calvary, established the New Covenant, which encompasses the covenants of the Old Testament, and carries even greater blessings and grace. Jesus was not born into a poor family. Joseph's family had social standing, material wealth, and a solid business. Poor people are never summoned to pay taxes. Joseph planned to rent a room at the inn; he wasn't looking for a handout. Joseph provided state of the art transportation (Cadillac Escalade of the day) for his bride. He had sufficient money to finance a trip to Egypt that lasted until the death of Herod (Luke 2:1-7). Jesus used a treasurer (John 13:29). Right thinking will suggest that there is no need for a treasurer unless there are enough funds to require a manager. Jesus dressed well such that the Roman soldiers recognized the value of his tailor-made coat and refused to divide it into pieces. Instead they gambled for it (John 19:23-24).

The early church was in wealth (Acts 4:33-35). They formed a society that was totally void of any lack, or poverty. Paul was wealthy. He promised in writing to pay back all the wages that a runaway slave, named Onesimus, owed his master (Philemon 1:18-19).

All the seeds of Abraham derive their fruitfulness from the Covenant God made with him. If you have truly surrendered your life to Christ, you are indeed a seed of Abraham according to Galatians 3:29. You are, therefore, entitled to claim your fruitfulness through our LORD Jesus Christ.

## PRAYERS

1. Father, Thank You for giving me the mandate to be fruitful and to multiply, to replenish the earth and subdue it, and to exercise dominion over everything You created (Genesis 1:28).

2. Father, for your Name's sake and by the authority of Your Word, may I begin to bear fruit, in Jesus' Name (Isaiah 37:31).

3. In the Name of Jesus, I declare that I am made in the image of my Father, Jehovah-Jireh, and in His likeness. My Father is fruitful, therefore I shall be fruitful, reproduce, increase, and multiply, in Jesus' Name (Genesis 1:26).

4. I am a seed of Abraham. Therefore, I shall be exceedingly fruitful (in my marriage, spiritually, financially, etc.), in Jesus' Name (Genesis 17:6).

5. In the Name of Jesus, I shall be like a tree planted by the rivers of water that bringeth forth its fruit in its season (Psalms 1:3).

6. Thank You, Covenant keeping God. My fruitfulness will bring glory to Your Holy Name, in Jesus' Name (1 Corinthians 10:31).

# DAY 10

# THY KINGDOM COME

*"Thy kingdom come, Thy will be done in earth, as it is in heaven" (Matthew 6:10).*

We are at war, and every child of the King has been recruited to fight in God's army. There is nothing we can do to escape it. We are not only born into God's army when we each gave our lives to Jesus, we were born [again] for enlistment in it. There is no demilitarized zone. Every area of endeavor is covered in this battle – no one can wish or pray it away. It extends from the spiritual realm, to the realm of the mind, and into the physical realm. Every issue of life is covered: health, family, finance, ministry, career, and more. Everything and everywhere is a battleground. Therefore, "Thy Kingdom come" implies:

"Thy" - God's will, not mine. "Kingdom" - rule of a King! Place of ruling! Establishing sovereignty on earth! "Come" –to become, to come to pass, to be done, to happen!

The good news is that we are not fighting for victory,

rather we are fighting in victory (Philippians 2:9-11). There is the supernatural world that is headed by God and His Kingdom personnel (Hebrews 12:22-24). There is also the supernatural world headed by Satan and his cohorts (Ephesians 6:12). Every man on earth is a member or citizen of either of these two worlds or kingdoms. Any agreement, transaction or covenant that is entered by, or on behalf of any man with any of the two kingdoms, brings the man under the laws, principles, and operations of that kingdom. God's program involves the rule of righteousness.

1. "Thy Kingdom come" is a cry for God to advance and expand that Kingdom in the hearts of people; converting the hearts of unbelievers and drawing people to a saving knowledge of Christ. It also means we are anticipating the day when that Kingdom literally comes, that is, when Jesus returns. It is a Kingdom that is both present and is to come; it is here and now, and will one day come in fullness. So, our prayer this day is, "Thy Kingdom Come!"

2. "Thy Kingdom come" is an evangelistic prayer. It is a call for God to increase His Kingdom on earth. We are a part of the answer to this prayer of ours. We have a role in bringing God's Kingdom to completeness. We need to pray for revival. God will answer this prayer through us by bringing people into His Kingdom as we share the Good News that Jesus saves. Many years ago, New England was the scene of the Great Awakening, a time of tremendous, effectual evangelism as the Holy Spirit moved through the land with great power.

3. "Thy Kingdom come" is a protest prayer. We are opposing every worldview that is contrary to God. Prayer is political action and social energy. David Wells, of Gordon-Conwell Seminary, calls this kind of prayer a "refusal to accept as normal what is pervasively abnormal (same sex bathrooms, breast feeding inside church sanctuary, prayer out of schools, divorce among pastors, abortion now termed human rights, lying now termed alternate truth, etc. This cannot continue on our watch." Why don't we pray more? God wants us to process our strong feelings about life, society, community, homes, etc. through prayer.

4. "Thy Kingdom come" is also a warfare prayer, a battle cry. How come everyone is not bowing before the hallowed Name of Jesus? Because there is another kingdom - the kingdom of darkness. People are enticed and enslaved by sin; this is the very essence of human predicaments. Our desire as Christians is for God to be honored and revered, so that even lawful captives can be set free (Isaiah 49:24-25). However, we are not unaware that there is enemy opposition to God's Kingdom. We are engaged in spiritual warfare as prayer warriors! Paul writes, "...our struggle is not against flesh and blood, but against the...powers of this dark world, and against the spiritual forces of evil in the heavenly realms" (Ephesians 6:12). God's wrath is certain, and His Truth is marching on. We will win, if we pray!

**Conclusion:** Whenever we pray, "Thy Kingdom Come," we indicate our desire for the dominion of God and the success of the Gospel. We have a Kingdom worth praying for. One day, the forces of evil will finally be routed by the hosts of heaven. In the meantime, pray, "Thy Kingdom come."

Our hearts' cry today is for God's Kingdom to come, we shall "fight the good fight of faith…" (1 Timothy 6:12).

- Saul fled from the battlefield and his name went into oblivion. There is no medal for yesterday's champion. You are as good as your last victory.

- Esau lost out on the battle of his destiny because he could not fight hunger.

- Samson could not fight against strange women, and he fell flat on his face and started dancing for the enemy of God.

- Joseph, on the other side, fought against sexual sin and moved up the ladder of God's purpose for his life.

It's your turn. Fight for your life. Fight for the destiny of your marriage. Fight for our youths in college campuses, pray that every Islamic agenda will be frustrated. Jesus' Kingdom must come, now!

## PRAYERS

1. Let us begin to thank God for this day. Thank Him for past victories and for the grace to approach the Throne of Mercy. Thank Him for Who He is, what He can do, and for whatever He has ever done for you.

2. Begin to plead the Blood of Jesus upon your life to redeem and cleanse you from every defilement of the spirit, soul, and body, in Jesus' Name.

3. Matthew 16:19 says, "I will give you the keys to the kingdom of heaven and whatever you shall bind on earth shall have been bound in heaven, and whatever you shall loose on earth shall have been loosed in heaven." Begin to scatter and terminate every conspiracy and confederacy against the church of the living God, against marriages, against our children, against the educational sector, etc., in Jesus' Name.

4. John Piper prayed saying, "God, grant me what I need to make Your Name great in the world." Pray it too! Every hand of the enemy stretched against men of God, against marriages, against the Body of Christ, must dry up, in Jesus' Name (1 Kings 13:4)

5. 1 Corinthians 4:20 says, "For the Kingdom of God does not consist in words, but in power." My Father, my Father, baptize me with your fire! Let your fire fall in my life, my church, my family, and my neighborhood today, O LORD! Empower me for victory, evangelism, prayer, etc.!

6. Every hijacker and terrorist on assignment that is monitoring my church, my destiny in life, and the evangelistic efforts of our church, be consumed by fire!

7. As from today, I prophesy that I shall experience revival. More souls shall be won into Jesus' Kingdom. There will be more open doors in the universities for campus fellowships, and for a prosperous, productive and fulfilling destiny, in Jesus' Name.

# DAY 11

# EXERCISING OUR DOMINION MANDATE

*"...Far above all principality, and power, and might, and dominion, and every name that is named, not only in this world, but also in that which is to come: And hath put all things under his feet, and gave him to be the head over all things to the church" (Ephesians 1:21-22).*

Welcome to another beautiful day. After praying that His Kingdom Come, He now mandates everyone to exercise His dominion mandate to "have what God said you can have and be what God said you can be." We are entering what the Bible calls the fullness of time, and much is at stake. God is positioning us to advance His kingdom into every realm held captive by the enemy. It is a full frontal, all out, now or never battle, and victory is guaranteed!

When God created man, He gave man dominion over everything on earth (Genesis 1:26-28). Unfortunately,

Adam fell out of favor and lost dominion when he disobeyed God. Christ Jesus is the perfect example of God's dominion restored onto humanity. When Jesus wanted to pay the temple tax, He only needed to command a fish to bring the money (Matthew 17:24-27). When Jesus was in the boat with the disciples and there was a storm, he spoke to the storm, and it obeyed him. I prophesy 'Peace, be still' in your lives in the Name of Jesus Christ, the Name that is above all names (Mark 4:35-41). Every sick person who came to Him went away healed. The lame walked, the blind saw, and the dead came back to life because He had dominion over death.

To be successful in this commission, we must understand fully our authority in Christ. That is, what some call "Kingdom authority" or "the dominion mandate." We must exercise dominion over sin (Romans 6:14), fear (1 John 1:7), the world (1 John 5:4-5), worries and anxieties (Philippians 4:6-7), demons (Ephesians 6:10-12), thoughts/imaginations (2 Corinthians 10:3-5), failures and setbacks (Micah 7:8).

You must know exactly what Jesus Christ's power is, and take dominion of the power He has given the church. Here are the principles outlined for you in the acrostic: D-O-M-I-N-I-O-N.

**D – Discover Your Source of Dominion.** We must understand the exceedingly great power we have through Jesus Christ. Jesus took the dominion from Satan, turned and gave the keys to the church (Matthew 16:18). We are a people of dominion.

**O – Obtain Knowledge on the Effective Use of Your Weapons.** Just as the conflict is spiritual, so are our weapons (2 Corinthians 10:3-5). Everyone that is going to walk in dominion must value PRAYER, LOVE, RIGHTEOUSNESS, and the WORD. Hide the Word in your heart, so that when an attack comes, you can use that double-edged sword (Ephesians 6:17; Hebrews 1:9).

**M – Maintain Your Relationship with the Body of Christ.** Christ's body is a living, moving entity. Stay close to the church (Colossians 1:18). We are in Christ Jesus, and He is in us. We are in the world but not of it (Ephesians 2:5).

**I – Identify Your Enemy.** How can you win a battle if you do not know who you are fighting? Identity begins with knowing who you are, and Whose you are in Christ. This gives security and confidence to fight the enemy in his territory (Acts 19:15).

**N –Never Be Unprepared.** Do not ever let your guard down (2 Corinthians 2:11). You are devil-proof by the blood of Jesus, so hold on to your weapons and never lay them down. Never take your eyes off Jesus (Hebrews 12:2).

**I –Imbibe the Spirit of Praise.** Learn how to use the weapon of praise. Punish the devil with your praise. God inhabits the praises of His people, so the devil cannot stand where He is being praised (Acts 16:25-26; Psalms 22:3).

**O – Obey the LORD Always.** Complete obedience to God is one of the keys to a life of dominion. We are ready to punish all disobedience only when our own obedience is perfect (2 Corinthians 10:5-6). Saul lost dominion over the nation of Israel because of his disobedience, and he was described as a rebellious person (1 Samuel 15:11-23).

**N – Never Share of His Glory.** God wants us to return all the glory back unto Him alone (1 Corinthians 1:29). Sharing of His glory will amount to pride on our own part. "God resists the proud, but gives grace to the humble" (1 Peter 5:5).

When God sends a word, it is like a seed which should be nurtured until it bears fruit, or else it will dry up and die. "And stay ye not, but pursue after your enemies, and smite the hindmost of them; suffer them not to enter into their cities: for the LORD your God had delivered them into your hand" (Joshua 10:19). The prophetic instruction that the soldiers should pursue their enemies not only spelt haste, it also implied a time-frame. The armies of God could not have afforded to wait all day before they started to pursue; the enemies would have escaped, and the promise could have expired. They had to act by hasty pursuit. Patience is a virtue, but procrastination is not; the two should not be confused. Delay could be disastrous when it comes to pursuing our enemies and taking back what is ours. There are prophecies one cannot afford to tarry over, otherwise they lose their relevance. Delay is dangerous when God says, "It is time to exercise the dominion mandate."

This is a call upon you and I to rise above mediocrity, sickness, poverty, sin, shame, etc., and to exercise our dominion mandate. We must bring honor, glory, and harvest to Christ's Kingdom. Take ownership of the right you have in Christ, and dominate in the Name of Jesus. As we move into our positions as righteous sons and daughters, we shall establish the dominion mandate everywhere we go, in Jesus' Name. "Then the righteous will shine like the sun in the kingdom of their Father" (Matthew. 13:43, NIV).

## PRAYERS

- Begin to sing Hallelujah to the LORD of Lords & King of kings. The 24 Elders fall before Him saying "Amen, blessing and glory and wisdom and thanksgiving and honor and power and might, be to our God forever and ever. Amen (Revelation 7:12).

- Plead the Blood of Jesus for cleansing and sanctification, and to overcome Satan and his demons (Revelation 12:11).

- Today, I receive fresh oil on my head (Psalms 92:10), and fresh fire on my altar of prayer in the Name of Jesus.

- O enemies, I pursue you this day by prayers, by fasting, by the Word, and by a life of righteousness. I cut off all your escape routes, and I begin to smite you, in Jesus' Name (Psalms 18:37-40).

- By the Holy Spirit, I demolish every work of the flesh in my life. I receive the grace for perfect obedience to my Commander in Chief, in Jesus' Name! I receive the power to say NO to sin and everything ungodly, in Jesus' Name!

- Father, I decree by Your authority, and by the power in the Name of Jesus, that all of my inheritance that has gone into the hands of the devil be returned to me NOW, in Jesus' Name. I will rule and reign in my domain, in Jesus' Name (Deuteronomy 2:24).

- Father make me a channel of blessings to my generation, in Jesus' Name.

- From today, I will begin to exercise dominion in every area of my life, by the authority in the Name of Jesus. Thank Him for prayers answered!

# DAY 12

# COMMANDING THE GATES

*"Lift up your heads, O ye gates; even lift them up, ye everlasting doors; and the King of glory shall come in" (Psalms 24:9).*

In spiritual warfare, one of the most important interpretations of 'gates' is that they constitute major barriers or obstacles to breakthroughs. Even the literal interpretation of 'gate' makes it clear that it is a barrier.

- Gates are frequently referred to in the Bible.

- The enemy erects gates to prevent the children of God from entering their destinies and possessions.

- One of your covenant rights as a seed of Abraham, and a born-again Christian, is expressly stated by God in Genesis 22:17 - "thy seed shall possess the gate of his enemies."

- In Revelation 3:7, Jesus is the key of David; He opens and no man shuts, and He shuts and no man opens. You need Jesus to permanently shut down every gate drawing afflictions and constant troubles into your life.

Shame is over, in Jesus' Name. Gates of favor, divine assistance, an sustenance are opened unto you today, in Jesus' Name.

- You cannot enter alone; the King of Glory must enter with you. Friends, enter with clean hands. What the LORD will start with you today, no power will stop, in Jesus' Name.

- The children of Israel were ready to possess Canaan, their God-given inheritance, but the gates of Jericho, a strategic city to the destiny of Israel, were shut (Joshua 6:1). "Now Jericho was straitly shut up because of the children of Israel: none went out, and none came in." The enemy knows that you have come to demand your breakthroughs today, but there is a gate he is shutting because of you. Get ready to bulldoze that gate right now, in the Name of Jesus.

- The enemy can also use gates to monitor people with the intent to harm them. In Judges 16:2-3, "And it was told the Gazites, saying, Samson is come hither. And they compassed him in, and laid wait for him all night in the gate of the city, and were quiet all the night, saying, In the morning, when it is day, we shall kill him. And Samson lay till midnight, and arose at midnight, and took the doors of the gate of the city, and the two posts, and went away with them, bar and all, and put them upon his shoulders, and carried them up to the top of a hill that is before Hebron." The Gazites heard that Samson was in town, so they camped there to monitor his movements. They sat there all night, planning to kill Samson at dawn. Instead, the Holy Ghost put them in a deep sleep.

Then, He awakened Samson in the middle of the night, who proceeded to uproot the entire foundation of the gate, and take it away. I prophesy over your life that every foundation of Satanic gates in your life will be uprooted this hour, in the Name of Jesus Christ!

Testimonies will begin to pour into your life after this day, in the Name of Jesus.

- Gates are used to lock people into prisons of stagnation, limitation, impossibility, and even death. Many have been condemned into the village of underdevelopment because the gates to the city of their breakthroughs have been shut. That was the case of Peter in Acts 12:10 - "When they were past the first and the second ward, they came unto the iron gate that leadeth unto the city; which opened to them of his own accord: and they went out, and passed on through one street; and forthwith the angel departed from him." When he was making his way to freedom, the Iron Gate that led to the city was there to stop him, but the Almighty God caused it to open supernaturally. Today, every Iron Gate to the city of your breakthrough shall open by itself, in the Name of Jesus.

- Lastly, as you get ready to fire, note that the glory wind of the LORD cannot blow in your direction until you command the ancient gates of pain to lift up their heads. Now cry out this confession: "Lift up your heads, O ye gates, even lift them up, ye everlasting doors, let the King of Glory come into (mention your name) life right now!"

# PRAYERS

1. Almighty God, I enter your gates with thanksgiving. Overshadow me with your presence, in Jesus' mighty Name. "Enter into His gates with thanksgiving, and into His courts with praise: be thankful and bless His Name (Psalms 100:4).

2. Thank You, Father, for opening before me the "two-leaved gates" of breakthrough, which shall never be shut, in the mighty Name of Jesus. "And the gates of it shall not be shut at all by day: for there shall be no night there" (Revelation 21:25).

3. Thank You, LORD, for blessing me with all spiritual blessings in heavenly places. I am redeemed by the blood of Jesus. I am an heir of God, and a joint heir with the LORD Jesus Christ. I confess, based on Galatians 3:29 that "I am in Christ, therefore, I am Abraham's seed and heir according to the promise."

4. Let the gate to the city of my breakthroughs be opened automatically, in the Name of Jesus.

5. Daniel possessed the gate of the King and sat there. The Iron Gate opened of its own accord to Peter. Samson uprooted the foundation of satanic gates in his life. Such will I experience, in the Name of Jesus.

6. I command every gate, shutting the Gospel from reaching my city, shutting the hearts of men from receiving Christ, locking people away from the altar of salvation, to lift up its head now, in the Name of Jesus.

7. O LORD, let every door of breakthrough You have opened to me remain opened. May the door of barrenness that you have shut remain shut from this day, in the Name of Jesus. "Thus saith the LORD to His anointed, to Cyrus, whose right hand I have holden, to subdue nations before him; and I will lose the loins of kings, to open before him the two leaved gates; and the gates shall not be shut" (Isaiah 45:1-2).

8. Thank you, LORD, for prayers answered, in Jesus' Name.

# DAY 13

# COMMANDING YOUR HARVEST

*"while the earth remaineth, seedtime and harvest, and cold and heat, and summer and winter, and day and night shall not cease" (Genesis 8:22).*

I welcome you to the day of commanding your harvest, in Jesus' Name. Genesis 8:22 states that "while the earth remaineth, seedtime and harvest, and cold and heat, and summer and winter, and day and night shall not cease." There is a season to sow, and harvest will come according to its season, or as the God of Harvest commands. What He said in Genesis 1:28, "Be fruitful, multiply…and have dominion," He's still saying today. Apostle Paul in Ephesians 3:20 uses three words to describe the power of God. The words are: 'Exceedingly,' 'abundantly,' and 'above.' These three words basically mean the same thing. They mean that the God of harvest is able to multiply exponentially what you ask, think or sow.

In Matthew 14:13-21, a boy sowed two fish and five loaves

of bread. When the disciples gave the two fish and five loaves of bread, which was "not enough" to Jesus, He multiplied the fish and loaves to the point that they fed every person there and had twelve baskets' leftovers. This is not mere addition, but multiplication. Expect multiplication this season in Jesus' Name.

The widow in 1 Kings 17 used the little flour and some oil to prepare a meal for Elijah. The widow did as Elijah asked, and Elijah ate all that she had. When all she had should have been gone, let's hear what happened: "And the barrel of meal wasted not, neither did the cruse of oil fail, according to the word of the LORD, which he spake by Elijah." (1 Kings 17:16). The God of harvest multiplied her flour and oil so she never went hungry again. The same God of harvest is visiting you today in Jesus' Name.

There are three types of people when discussing harvest:

1. The first are those that sow nothing, and they harvest nothing.

2. The second category are those that sow little; their harvest is always proportional to what they sow.

3. The third category are those that sow much, and they reap exponentially or in multiplications.

I want you to be aware that there are forces contending for those in the second category. The Bible states this fact in Matthew 13:25 – "But while men slept, his enemy came and sowed tares among the wheat, and went his way." According to this text, this man sowed. However, he did not receive a proportional harvest because of the work of the enemy. The result is profitless hard labor, sweat, unproductivity, discouragement, frustration, sorrow, sadness, failure, shame and disgrace. Why? He discovered the enemy has shot a deadly arrow at his harvest.

Matthew 13:27-28 (NLT), says, "The farmer's workers went to him and said, 'Sir, the field where you planted that good seed is full of weeds! Where did they come from?" An enemy has done this..., the farmer exclaimed". Whatever is contending with your harvest is not of God. You must fight against these enemies. Every arrow of the enemy directed towards the harvest of your sowing shall backfire and their machineries malfunction, in Jesus' Name. By the Power of the Holy Ghost, this season, the devourer shall be devoured, in Jesus' mighty Name.

*"But all who devour you will be devoured, and all your enemies will be sent into exile. All who plunder you will be plundered, and all who attack you will be attacked" (Jeremiah 30:16 (NLT).*

The widow in 2 Kings 4:5-6 obeyed the prophet. "So she did as she was told. Her sons kept bringing jars to her, and she filled one after another. Soon, every container was full to the brim! "Bring me another jar," she said to one of her sons. "There aren't any more!" he told her. And then the olive oil stopped flowing." God took the drops of oil and obedience given to the prophet and multiplied them. This is a great miracle for those in category three. Can you imagine if she had more vessels to pour into? She gathered vessels according to, and in proportion of her image of how big God was to her. Tell me, how do you see God? Harvest is coming to you today. Sow big and you'll reap exponentially, in Jesus' Name.

# PRAYERS

1. Father, Thank You for this new day, and for giving seed to the sower – good seeds: talents, wisdom, knowledge and potential to succeed and excel, in Jesus' Name.

2. I cancel every wicked, evil and secret plan of my adversary to make me work like an elephant and eat as a rat, in Jesus' Name.

3. O earth, earth, refuse to cooperate with the enemies of my harvest in Jesus' Name. I will not labor for others to harvest, build for others to inhabit and every strange power targeting my harvest, scatter by fire, in Jesus' Name.

4. Father cause me to sing a new song of good harvesters this day. I will sing and praise you my God for I will receive a hundredfold return on all my seeds, in Jesus' Name.

5. Every evil eye watching my harvest, receive blindness. Evil hands pointing at my harvest, dry up. Evil mouth speaking against my harvest, be silenced permanently, in Jesus' Mighty Name.

6. I decree and declare that I and the children the LORD has given me shall enjoy the good fruits of our labor, and shall leave a legacy of abundance, fruitfulness, and godly blessedness of God's kingdom for my next generation, in Jesus' Name.

7. Thank You LORD for prayers answered of exponential harvest of souls, finance and health. Thank You LORD for the joy and preservation of our harvest for your glory, in Jesus' Name.

# DAY 14

# TAKING OVER THE GATES OF THE ENEMY

*"Rise ye up, take your journey...behold, I have given into thine hand...his land: begin to possess it, and contend with him in battle" (Deuteronomy 2:24).*

*"...your [great enemy] the devil walks about like a roaring lion, seeking whom he may devour. Resist [the devil], steadfast in the faith..." (1 Peter 5:8-9).*

Life is truly a battlefield. A very fierce battle is raging over your soul, whether you are aware of the battle or not. As an individual, your desire to get involved in the battle, or a lack thereof, is irrelevant; the battle is on! (Revelation 12:12). Equally poignant is that your ignorance of, or indifference to this raging battle simply makes you an easy prey and a guaranteed victim in the battle. Every occurrence in this physical realm of the earth has a remote control; there are no happen-stances. The unpalatable mysteries and inexplicable experiences that you pass through on a regular basis testify to the ongoing battle. We must, in holiness, confront and contend with the enemy of our souls that we may take over these gates in battle, by praying strategically under the unction of the Holy Ghost.

The Bible acknowledges the reality of this lifelong warfare. It says, "...we do not wrestle against flesh and blood..." (Ephesians 6:12), and therefore commands us to "...fight the good fight of faith..." (1 Timothy 6:12). The Bible advises us to "...endure hardship as a good soldier..." (2 Timothy 2:3-4). We are reminded that the battle we are in is essentially spiritual in the portion which says, "For though we walk in the flesh, we do not war after the flesh. For the weapons of our warfare are not carnal..." (2 Corinthians 10:3-5). The battle is real. It is raging. It is decisive. Its outcome is what manifests as your daily experiences.

Consequently, the "business as usual" mindset is no longer acceptable. Jesus' mandate in Matthew 28:19-20 must be carried out with understanding, commitment, speed and strategy. We must possess the gates of our enemies as promised to Abraham in Genesis 22:17. Unlike Abraham's time, however, these gates are not as perceptible or as clearly defined. Godly wisdom informs the realization that the enemy's gates we are up against are Government, Media, Education, Economy, Religion, Arts and Entertainment, and Family/Homestead. These are the gates we must capture, because these are the mind-molders of the society and the enemy has set his battle in array, ready for a fight with whosoever challenges his authority. For a while now, the church has ignored these gates or sectors of the society because we assumed they belonged to the devil.

God spoke extensively to Moses and Israel about the Promised Land he had planned for them. However, they had to overcome seven nations greater than them. Those physical nations had spiritual implications in the marketplace. The seven nations were the Hittites, the Girgashites, the Amorites, the Canaanites, the Perizzites, the Hivites and the Jebusites (Deuteronomy 7:1). Just as in the times of old, the Church is faced with seven of the enemy's gates as previously detailed above. These seven gates must come under the control of the redeemed of the LORD (Deuteronomy 7:21-23). We must declare what the LORD told Zerubbabel in Zechariah 4:7; "Who art thou, O great mountain? Before Zerubbabel thou shalt become a plain..." We are going to pray strategically in pulling down the enemy's gates and possessing the land.

These are the gates and the representation of each in the marketplace:

1.  **The gate of Media (the Hittites):** These are news outlets that create and report news of fear, terror, plagues, disease, war, etc. We need to capture this gate to control the media in every nation, so we can spread the good news (Philippians 4:8; Isaiah 52:7).

2.  **The gate of Government & Politics (the Girghashites):** This gate is the most strategic because it establishes laws and decrees that affect and control other gates. Examples are the LGBT agenda, legalization of abortion, etc (Isaiah 14:12-16; Proverbs 14:34-35, 29:2).

3.  **The gate of Education (the Amorites):** Humanism

81

and godlessness are the philosophies of this gate (2 Timothy 3:1-5). The Church of Jesus Christ must step in to begins to teach and live out the undiluted truth of God's Word (2 Timothy 4:1-5; Proverbs. 22:6).

4. **The gate of Economy (the Canaanites):** This is the gate of wealth or money and the systems of its production, distribution and consumption (Luke 16:13; 1 Timothy 6:10). The word of God concerning His Church is recorded in 2 Chronicles 2:20. God is still looking for the 'Josephs', 'Elijahs', and the 'Elishas' of our time.

5. **The gate of Religion (the Perizzites):** It is the religious spirit assigned to steal the worship designated for God. It thrives on lies and carnality. This gate must be invaded by true, Spirit-filled worship (John 4:21-24) and strategic prayers guided by diligent spiritual mapping.

6. **The gate of Arts & Entertainment (the Hivites):** This gate includes the arts, music, sports, fashion, and entertainment in homes & movie theaters. Our God is the God of creativity, pleasure and joy (Psalms 16:11). Many Christian artists no longer associate with the church. Most have turned their backs on the mandate of using their talents to bring down the glory of God (2 Chronicles 5:11-14).

7. **The gate of Family/Homestead (the Jebusites):** The family unit is under serious assault by Satan (2 Timothy 3:1-4). The social ills that spring out of the rejection of Biblical injunctions include fear, depression, addictions, and violence. The good news is that God

has the perfect remedy for the family since it is His brain child to begin with (Malachi 4:6; Obadiah 1:17).

It has always been the will of God for His covenanted children to possess the gates of their enemies (Deuteronomy 1:8). We need to rise up today to possess the gates of media, economy, religion, government, education, arts & entertainment, and the family/homestead (Deuteronomy 7:1-2; 16-23; Numbers 14:6-9).

## PRAYERS

1. Let us begin by thanking God for creating this day, week, and month for our pleasures. Thank Him for helping you thus far in your journey with Him.

2. To those building or repairing these gates of the enemy, your ministry is terminated in my life, family, church, community as from today, in Jesus' Name.

3. Whatever the devil is holding unto as a legal right to keep me bound, Holy Ghost Fire, consume it now; Blood of Jesus, release me, in Jesus' Name.

4. Every power that is defying, ignoring and challenging the gifts and grace of God upon my life, be consumed now by fire, in Jesus' Name.

5. Every garment of oppression and affliction that I am wearing about, forced upon me in the spirit realm, tear now by fire, in Jesus' Name.

6. We take back all the territories the enemy has illegally stolen and mandate a sevenfold restoration, in Jesus' Name (Proverbs 6:31)

7. Begin to thank God for prayers answered.

# RELEASING THE FOUR CARPENTERS OF HEAVEN

*"… And the LORD shewed me four carpenters. Then said I, what come these to do? And he spake, saying, these are the horns which have scattered Judah, so that no man did lift up his head: but these are come to fray them, to cast out the horns of the Gentiles, which lifted up their horn over the land of Judah to scatter it"* (Zechariah 1:20-21).

Welcome to the day of the mystery of the number 'FOUR' of 'Complete Restoration.' What is the significance of the number four? It is the number of stability, order, and completion of justice. There are four cardinal points that indicate directions: North, East, West, and South. We also have expressions like, "the four corners of the earth" (Isaiah 11:11-12). There are four phases of the moon and four seasons, namely: Summer, Winter, Fall and Spring. In the World, we have four elements: earth, air, fire, and water. Jesus was nailed and hung on a cross, after which Roman soldiers divided up his clothes into four parts (one for each soldier - John 19:23). There are four gospel accounts of Jesus' life and ministry. Today, the four angelic carpenters shall bring order and stability into your life, in Jesus' Name.

One of the great provisions of God for the prosperity, distinction, and dominion of the saints on earth is the angels. They fight the saints' battles. And they don't lose any battle they engage in (2 Kings 19:35; Acts 12:21-23). Angels are not to be worshipped by men, they are emissaries of God to man. They are but messengers, not masters over man; for men are superior to angels before God because we are His image bearers. (1 Corinthians 6:3)

There are four forces we need to fight, and they are mentioned in Ephesians 6:12 namely:

- rulers
- authorities
- powers of this dark world and
- spiritual forces of evil in heavenly realms.

Each of these four forces is called a strongman, or a stronghold because the devil works through them. Therefore, whenever the devil attacks, he reinforces each attack with his spiritual forces of evil to ensure the victim does not survive the attack. These ungodly forces are horns that scatter; they seek only to destroy anyone they come against. So many lives have been scattered and put in a state of disarray today by the operations of the horns of wickedness. But today, those horns of wickedness working against you shall be scattered, in Jesus' Name. The angelic carpenters of heaven are ready to roll away demonic stones that are planted on the doorways of man's breakthrough (Matthew 28:2). They shut the mouths of the devouring lions of life (Daniel 6:22); they open prison doors, and loosen chains without keys (Acts 5:18-19, 12:7-10); they perform things that are inexplicable and unimaginable to us as humans.

The horns that scattered Judah (praise, testimony, laughter, joy) in your life shall be scattered today in Jesus' Name. Every demonic horn assigned to scatter what God is building in your life, family, ministry, and home shall be scattered, in Jesus' Name. Zechariah 1:19 says that the horns have a game plan to scatter Judah, then Israel, (the prince of God-assigned to rule, be strong, have authority over), and then proceed to Jerusalem (city of peace, abundance, city of God). That's a lie. They will NOT succeed, in Jesus' Name. Closed doors are about to be reopened, your captivity is about to turn; difficulties, hardness and struggles are about to melt away from your life. You are about to command and enjoy the services and ministrations of the four carpenters of heaven in every area of your life from now.

Besides the weapons of the Name of Jesus, the Blood of Jesus, and the Word of God, another great weapon is to have the carpenters of heaven engage their hammers on our behalves. With these hammers, Satan and his cohorts are rendered ineffective. The horn of their power and authority is destroyed. I believe God with you today that God will engage His divine carpenters (angels on assignment) to fight the battles of your life, in Jesus' Name. Every horn of wickedness against you and your family shall be scattered and cast out if you will be ready to pray aggressively, forcefully, and prevailingly, provoking your angel into action, in Jesus' Name.

## PRAYERS

1. Father, I Thank You for today, the day of deploying the carpenters of heaven to fight my battles. Thank You because I am more than a conqueror through Jesus that loved me (1 John 4:4). Thank You that I am not fighting for victory, but fighting in victory.

2. Father, wherever demonic rulers, demonic authorities, or powers of this dark world have been ruling over me, preventing me from rising, I invoke the Blood of Jesus Christ against them, in Jesus' Name. Let the hammer of the carpenters of heaven hit them hard, in Jesus' Name.

3. Father, in any area of my life that I have come under the attack of the spiritual forces of darkness in heavenly places, let the Blood of Jesus fight for me and bring me victory, in Jesus' Name. Father, let the carpenters of heaven scatter them with their hammers, in Jesus' Name.

4. Thou, angel of the living God sent to assist me, begin to breakdown every prison wall that is caging my destiny. Contend with my Herod to cancel every death sentence that is meant for me right now.

5. Ye four carpenters of heaven, arise on my behalf and turn my problems and challenges to promotion; bring waters for me from the deserts of my dream, business, marriage, ministry, career, finances, etc., in Jesus' Name.

# DAY 16

# ABOVE AND BEYOND

*"Now unto him that is able to do exceeding abundantly above all that we ask or think, according to the power that worketh in us" (Ephesians 3:20)*

Howdy, brothers and Sisters in Christ! I'm excited about God every day, and hearing from Him gives me the assurance that I am still His. Our theme two days ago was 'Commanding your Harvest.' Yesterday, it was 'Greatness by Covenant', and today, our theme will be 'Above and Beyond'. I think God is up to something for His obedient children. You will not miss out on this outpouring of the bounty from heaven, in Jesus' Name.

Ephesians 3:20 (NKJV), says, "Now to Him who is able to do exceeding, abundantly above all that we ask or think, according to the power that works in us."

**Definition of terms:** Above implies higher in rank, authority or power; to be in heaven on earth; to be overhead or upstairs. Beyond also implies to be superior, surpassing, beyond comprehension, etc. In Ephesians 3, we read about the mysteries of the church. We are told that we would be the same body and partakers of His promise together in Christ who redeemed us. Paul ends his explanations, revelations and prayers with a doxology (praise and worship) in Ephesians 6. Paul is desperate for you and me to know something that we do not know about Him. See how Paul describes the character of God in his opening phrase of Ephesians 3:20 - It is "now, unto Him...."

1.  **The "Now-ness" of God:** God is always NOW! He asked Moses, "thus shall thou say unto the children of Israel, I AM hath sent me unto you" (Exodus 3:14). "He is the same yesterday, today and forever" (Hebrews 13:8). He is always standing ready to perform His character and good- ness. He is never depleted of His ability to perform. Make no mistake of who He is talking about. This is the capital "H" in Him. Talking about the LORD God Almighty, the LORD Mighty in Battle, El-Shaddai – this is the God who is above all gods, the LORD of all LORDs, King of all kings. He cannot be challenged. Expect more from Him today.

2.  **The Able "bility" of God:** He is able to do. God has inherent power (Dunamai). He has inherent power in Himself to do what He wants, when He wants, how He wants and as long as He wants. He needs no permission from anyone. He is able to answer all the prayers of the over 7.6 billion people on earth at the same time with precision and accuracy. He has inexhaustible power, grace and mercy to answer all the prayers of what we ask or think, abundantly and above.

Please don't overlook the 'do'. God is able to not simply talk about it, nor just able to think about it; He is able to DO it. He is able to perform, complete, finish, uphold and defend what He has promised.

God's intent is to grant your request. He does not need to get anyone's permission to bless you. He does not need to check with anyone before downloading His grace upon your life. He is willing and able to do what you request of Him.

3. **That Hidden Attitude (service: above and beyond):** There is a hidden attitude found in the scripture that I noticed in several other Bible accounts. This attitude impresses God. It moves God like our faith moves Him. It brings God to the edge of His seat when He sees His children behave in this way:

- Rebecca, the wife of Isaac, lived a beautiful life of service. She never dreamed how her serving heart would open the greatest doors of her life, but she discovered that serving opens doors of destiny. We read the account in Genesis 24:18-20. The well was deep (it takes around 50 steps to descend to the water) and a camel could drink 25 gallons of water in one sitting. Ten camels make for 250 gallons. If she could carry 5 gallons, it would take her up to 50 trips. When the heart is willing, service is impelled and not compelled; agreeable, and not disagreeable; executing rather than excusing. She did the job well and finished what she started. Yes, her service was not convenient.

No wonder she was blessed above and beyond. She became the great grandmother of our LORD Jesus Christ.

- Solomon went above and beyond in his offering to God. "And Solomon went up there to the bronze altar before the LORD, which was at the tabernacle of meeting, and offered a thousand burnt offerings on it," (1 Chronicles 1:6) See what the God of above and beyond did: "wisdom and knowledge are granted to you; and I will give you riches and wealth and honor, such as none of the kings have had who were before you, nor shall any after you have the like" (2 Chronicles 1:12).

- Peter yielded his ship (Luke 5:1-7). Why would Jesus need a mortal's ship? Did the Great God have to ask a mere man for his ship? Wasn't that moment a unique opportunity to display his greatness to stand mid-air above the waters to preach the mysteries of God? The better question today is "Do I have a ship He might need today? Could that partnership be the key to ending the reproaches of a protracted night?" Peter did the extraordinary service to get the above and beyond blessing of ship-sinking, net-breaking break- through (Luke 5:7). I pray for you today, that may your many past pains never kill your sensitivity to other hurting people, who are still where you were, in Jesus' Name.

Listen, 'nothing goes for nothing' – no service, no blessing! I dare you today to go above and beyond in your service, offering, prayers, worship and obedience, and let's see what the "Now" and "Able" God will do for you and yours this day.

## PRAYERS

1. I praise You O LORD. You are Jehovah-Jireh (The Great Provider). You are El-Shaddai (the All Sufficient God). The Greatest, the 'Now' God. The only One who has the ability to perform, complete, finish, uphold and defend what He has promised. Receive our worship and praise, O LORD.

2. Every agenda, programming and transactions of the enemy into my future, any sin or iniquity in my life, blood of Jesus, annul and cancel it in Jesus' Name. Father forgive me all my sins and clothe me with new raiment, in Jesus' Name.

3. Father, I receive the attitude of service to go above and beyond in my prayer life, worship life, giving, assisting people, serving God, etc. like Rebecca, Solomon and Peter today, in Jesus' Name.

4. Father, I know there is good in the land. As from today, let the earth yield unto me its finest products in Jesus' Name. I will no longer eat the leftover of the earth, in Jesus' Name.

5. Father, fill my cup with your abundance. Let my cup run over, in Jesus' Name.

**SING:** *I give myself away, I give myself away, so You can use me/2ce. Here I am, Here I stand, LORD, my life is in your hands, LORD, I'm longing to see Your desires revealed in me:* by William McDowell.

## DAY 17

# EAGLE BELIEVERS SOARING

*"As an eagle stirreth up her nest, fluttereth over her young, spreadeth abroad her wings, taketh them, beareth them on her wings: So the Lord alone did lead him, and there was no strange god with him. He made him ride on the high places of the earth, that he might eat the increase of the fields; and he made him to suck honey out of the rock, and oil out of the flinty rock; Butter of kine, and milk of sheep, with fat of lambs, and rams of the breed of Bashan, and goats, with the fat of kidneys of wheat; and thou didst drink the pure blood of the grape" (Deuteronomy 32:11-14).*

God is asking you to begin to soar. You will be soaring every phase of your life, in Jesus' Name. It is amazing to see so many wonderful references about the eagle. Mountains, rivers, storms, clouds, and the rain pose no problem for the eagle because it has strong wings. No wonder the LORD spoke so much about the eagle in the Bible, probably more than any other bird known to man, and God called you an eagle, the king of all birds.

In reading through the passages of Scripture, one can see that it is the Grace of God that saves Israel. It is the same Grace that saves us as believers in our present day walk with the LORD. Salvation, then and now, is by the grace of God alone! In Exodus 19:4, God reminded the nation of Israel about their rescue from slavery. He rescued them by His great strength and brought them to Himself. It was not their strength, intellect, connections or military might that liberated them. No! As God rescued the Israelites from 430 years of slavery in Egypt, so He desires to rescue us out of our sin into eternal life. If we will turn away from our sinful lives and ask Him to save us, He will do so.

1. **Our Father God is an Eagle:** An eagle cannot beget a vulture. Like begets like. "As many as received Christ, He gave power to become Sons of God" (John. 1:12.) If God our Father is an Eagle and we are born again children of God, we cannot be ducks.

2. **The Eagle is a symbol of God and of Deity.** The grandeur and grace of the eagle in flight are well-known. Even at rest, the eagle's size, power, shoulders, and furrowed brow give it a regal pose. In Ezekiel 1:10 & 10:4, the deity is represented by the face of an eagle. In Revelation 4:7,14, the deity is pictured as a flying eagle. The eagle is the jet fighter of the bird family.

3. **We have an Eagle Savior:** "For Moses truly said unto the fathers, A prophet shall the LORD your God raise up unto you of your brethren, like unto me; Him shall ye hear in all things whatsoever He shall say unto you" (Acts 3:22). Jesus came as our Eagle savior and Hebrews 2:11 records that, "He is not ashamed to call us

94

brethren;" we are his siblings. We are like the eagle and we are ordained to soar in the sky, not struggle on earth. I pray that you will receive impartation to soar! Romans 8:29-30," For whom He did foreknow, He also did predestinate to be conformed to the image of His Son, that He might be the firstborn among many brethren. Moreover, whom He did predestinate, them He also called: and whom He called, them He also justified: and whom He justified, them He also glorified." We Are Eagles By Redemption:

- Redeemed to Walk in Dominion: Genesis 1:28; Numbers 23:23; Isaiah 8:8.

- Ordained to Be Salt of The Earth and Light of The World: Matthew 5:6; Obadiah 1:21.

- We Are Redeemed as Kings to Reign on Earth: Revelation 5:9-10.

- We Are Redeemed to Be Fruitful, Not Barren: Psalms 128:1-5; Isaiah 5:1-13; Psalms 1:3.

- We Are Redeemed to Be Greater Than All Old Testament Saints: Matthew 11:11.

- We Are Redeemed to Manifest Seven Redemptive Treasures: Revelation 5:12 says: "...Lamb that was slain to receive power, and riches, and wisdom, and strength, and honor, and glory, and blessing."

- We Are Supernatural Beings: Psalms 82:6.

## Characteristics of Eagles that we must demonstrate as Believers:

1. They are creatures satisfied with few neighbors: If an eagle must keep company, it would be with fellow eagles that can fly as high and as fast as itself. Eagles typically have no business with any other bird, flightless or otherwise. Most of the time, the great eagles fly alone. You, as an eagle must be selective of the company you keep. You need to be in covenant only with people with the same burden, vision and passion as yourself. Chickens, owls, bats, and ostriches cannot understand nor flow with them.

2. They are creatures accustomed to deep quietness: Because eagles most often fly alone and soar to such great heights, they are accustomed to deep [unbroken] quietness (Isaiah 30:15; Job 39:27-29). The LORD expects us to come up high like the eagle, but also to learn to dwell before Him in deep quietness so we can hear His still small Voice speak to us (Isaiah 40:31).

3. They are creatures accustomed to the "Ways of the Wind": The eagle does not do a lot of flying as it predominantly travels by soaring on wind gusts traveling upward where it desires to go (Isaiah 40:31). To do this effectively, the eagle must learn to study the wind and its patterns, which means it must learn to wait and watch (Psalms 27:13-14).

4. They are creatures that live above the clouds: When pursued, the eagle flies vertically skyward, heading for the sun. There are two major reasons for this tactic. One, it is heading home to where it lives above the

clouds (Psalms 121:1-2). Two, not many birds can look directly at the sun like the eagle can. If they attempt to, they go blind, which renders them useless as a predator to the eagle who does not break stride.

5. They are creatures that sight the rising of the sun before others: Eagles sight the rising of the sun before others because they dwell above the clouds. The rising of the sun is important; it's a signifier of a new day. The LORD Jesus will return without announcement and only those who are on the lookout for His coming will see Him (John 14:1-3; Acts 1:11; Matthew 24:27).

6. They are creatures that dominate huge expanses of land (territory): An eagle's outlined territory is useful for sourcing food for itself and its young. It is an efficient and fearsome hunter (Job 9:26). The eagle has very sharp eyes which can see 5 miles: forward, sideways and backwards. It is distinctly gifted to see the size of a quarter from about 5 miles away. The territory is also needed for the training of its young when the time comes for them to leave the nest (Genesis 18:19; Proverbs 22:6). The young are dropped from great heights in the coaching process. The eagle prefers that no predator runs off with its young.

7. They are creatures that must not be eaten yet they can eat any animal: Of all the LORD God has given man to eat, the eagle is not one of them (Deuteronomy 14:12). The LORD has set you apart as one consecrated for His use and glory alone. This does not mean the enemy will not desire to kill, steal, and destroy you; it simply means you have the assurance from the Sovereign One that He Is in control of all that concerns

you (Psalms 105:15; 2 Kings 1:10).

8. As you seek God with passion, you will not eat leftovers or filthy things. God will make you to rise like an eagle, in Jesus' Name.

# PRAYERS

1. Father, let the world see Your greatness, power, glory and mighty acts in my life, in Jesus' Name. "Ye have seen... (Exodus 19:4)"

2. Father, as the eagle beareth her young away from danger, deliver me from danger, enslavement and bondage.

3. Father, as the eagles soar upon the current of winds, let me overcome every restriction to my progress, in Jesus' Name.

4. Father, as the eagles overcome the power of storms, I overcome every storm on the path of my destiny, by a mighty act of God, in Jesus' Name.

5. Father, as the eagles beareth her young ones and protect them from danger in her nest:

6. I command divine protection over my life, in Jesus' Name.

7. I command divine provision over my life, in Jesus' Name.

8. I command angelic care over my life, in Jesus' Name. Father, in the order of deliverance from Egypt, I receive redemption from calamity, sorrow and disappointment.

9. Father, let me soar high like an eagle.

# DAY 18

# GREATNESS BY COVENANT

*"And said, By myself have I sworn, saith the Lord, for because thou hast done this thing, and hast not withheld thy son, thine only son: That in blessing I will bless thee, and in multiplying I will multiply thy seed as the stars of the heaven, and as the sand which is upon the sea shore; and thy seed shall possess the gate of his enemies; And in thy seed shall all the nations of the earth be blessed; because thou hast obeyed My voice"* (Genesis 22:16-18).

Today, by covenant, you shall be great, in the Name of Jesus. One of the key words that unlocks the Bible is 'Covenant'. The Bible is a story of covenants; covenant between God and human beings. A covenant is an agreement between two or more people promising to do certain things, or fulfill certain obligations or promises under certain conditions, and the course of action is bound. A covenant is usually between two unequal partners: a weak person and a strong person; a poor person and a rich person. In covenants, the power of the strong is made available to the weak and the weak transfers his weakness to the strong. A covenant is different from a contract. In a contract, if either fails in his obligation, the other party is free from the contract, and it's always bilateral with two equal parties.

A marriage is a covenant. The Last Will and Testament is a covenant. God's relationship with man is always based on a conditional or unconditional covenant. The bible is divided into two sections called the old and New Testaments (Covenant). Our God is a Covenant making God. God, the Almighty, All-Sufficient and All-knowing, made a covenant with a weak and fallible man. God has put himself on obligation with man. Our God is also a covenant-keeping God. The greatness of the Jewish race, both past and present generations, can be directly traced to the covenants God made with their ancestors. Each time they keep the covenant, blessings follow for them and their children, but each time they break the covenants, they incur some punishments.

God made a covenant of greatness with Abraham, Isaac and Israel. The weaker ought to take on the name of the stronger. For instance, the wife takes the last name of the husband. However, with God, the reverse is true – the stronger taking the name of the weaker. God is known as the God of Abraham, Isaac and Israel.

In Genesis 15:18, the Bible says, "on the same day, the LORD made a covenant with Abraham saying "to your descendants I have given this land." In Genesis 17: 1-9, God affirmed the covenant, stated the content of the covenant, the basis for its continuous enjoyment, and how it shall become trans-generational. Genesis 17:19 says, "...I will establish my covenant with him for an everlasting covenant and with his descendants after him." Now, when Abraham kept his side of the covenant, we see God blessing Abraham, Isaac his son, and the descendants of Isaac according to His Word.

In Genesis 22: 16-18, God made a covenant of greatness with Abraham and his descendants; "...because you have done this thing, and have not withheld your son, your only son, blessing I will bless you, and multiplying I will multiply your descendants as the stars of the heaven, and as the sand which is on the seashore; and your descendants shall possess the gate of their enemies. In your seed all the nations of the earth shall be blessed, because you have obeyed my voice."

The natural Jewish race from Abraham until the present generation.

## JEWISH STATISTICS (2009)

According to Steven Silbiger, in "The Jewish Phenomenon: Seven Keys to the Enduring Wealth of a People" , The Jews and their descendants have more intellectuals, millionaires and billionaires living in our generation than any other race or people group in the world per capita.

Total Jewish population 13–14 million or 0.2% of the world population as of 2009. Officially, 5.4 million Jews live in Israel while 5.3 million live in the United States, and the rest are scattered in other countries of the world.

## World Wealth and Riches

Though 0.2% of world population, the Jews and their descendants have produced 25%, or one fourth of Forbes 500 richest billionaires in the world as of 2009.

33% or one third of the world's richest men are Jewish.

## Jews in the United States

Though 1.7% of American population, they produced officially, 48% of American billionaires.

## Jews in Russia

Though 0.5% of the population (in the 1990s), they Produced about 90% of the Russian financial oligarchs.

With these very interesting statistics, there are four factors responsible for this greatness:

1. Covenants connection: (Genesis 17:18; Galatians 3:29).
2. Obedience to Biblical injunctions: (Isaiah 1:19; John 2:5).
3. Culture of hard work: (Proverbs 12:27; Romans 12:11)
4. Persecution and suffering: (Mark 10:30; 1 Peter 5:10).

Since the Bible says that God is no respecter of person (Acts 10:34), neither does he show partiality (Galatians 3:11), anyone that lives under the Abrahamic covenant covering, and willing to apply these principles, can benefit under the covenant of great- ness, and have benefited from it.

# CHRIST: OUR COVENANT CONNECTION

Galatians 3:29 says: "If you are Christ's, then you are Abraham's seed, and heirs according to the promise" (of greatness). By this Scripture, a born-again child of God automatically comes under the Abrahamic covenant covering. So, it is not a coincidence that the rich people in our generation have Jewish backgrounds.

I have good news for someone today. God is about to take you to the class of the greats in your generation because of your covenant connection to Abraham through our LORD Jesus Christ. Your story will be the next among the greats that your generation will read, in Jesus' Name.

## PRAYERS

1. Father, I Thank You for my covenant connection to Abraham through my acceptance of the Jesus Christ as my LORD.

2. Father, I Thank You for preparing me, and giving me the revelation of greatness.

3. Father, I Thank You that you are not a respecter of persons, neither do you take bribe, nor show partiality.

4. Thank You for provoking me at this time to desire greatness using the accomplishments of great people in the past and present generations.

5. I receive the divine ability to become great according to my desire and your plans for me, in Jesus' Name.

6. If you made Abraham, Isaac and Jacob great, you can make me great and I shall be great, in Jesus' Name.

7. You made Isaac great by his biological connection to Abraham. Make my children great by their biological connection to me and covenant connection to Christ, in Jesus' Name.

8. I receive the grace for diligence that will elevate me to the status of the great, in Jesus' Name.

9. I prophesy in the Name of Jesus that I shall be great, my children shall be great, and their offspring shall be great as well, in Jesus' Name. Amen.

**SING:** *Verily/5x the LORD said to me, I shall be great, I shall be lifted, it shall be well with me.*

# DAY 19

# THE COMEBACK

*"... And the LORD turned the captivity of Job, when he prayed for his friends: also, the LORD gave Job twice as much as he had before" (Job 42:10)*

I welcome you to the day of 'THE COMEBACK.' The Bible is a book of comebacks. It is a book of hope, encouragement and new perspective. God is in the business of giving fresh starts to people. Today, hope shall be released to seemingly hopeless situations, direction to the directionless, and help to the needy. It does not matter what you are going through, it does not matter what you are up against in your life, ministry, home, and nation. Today, I will hear you say, "Jesus, the God of comebacks, has done it for me." God is always good and His plans of good will always prevail regardless what our plans were. (Jeremiah 29:11).

Adam and Eve were in paradise in the Garden of Eden until they believed a lie (Genesis 2-3). It is the same lie that we believe today, that God was withholding something good from them. After they ate the forbidden fruit, they lost it all. They needed a comeback, God offered them a comeback because God loved, cared for, blessed, and sustained them. In Genesis 6-9, Noah built a big boat, gathered all the animals two by two, and saved humanity. Right after Noah and his family escaped the judgment of God, he planted a vineyard, got drunk and caused a big conflict in his family. However, God gave him a comeback, which we read in Hebrews 11:7, where it is noted that Noah became an heir of righteousness in keeping with his faith.

Job 14:7 says, " For there is hope of a tree, if it be cut down, that it will sprout again, and that the tender branch thereof will not cease." Expectations shall become manifestations today in Jesus' Name. As long as you are in His grip, do not count yourself out. Your case may already be dead and stinking (John. 11:39); you may be on life support now, or your case might have already been declared closed. I say you are coming back!

People thought it was over for Job when he faced a bubonic plague that devastated him. He lost everything: estate, children, health, and other prized possessions. Job's wife thought it was over. She encouraged her husband to curse God and die (Job 2:9). Friend, never curse God for whatever you are going through. It may take time, but you will get out. The God of comeback did not say it was over because He has the final say. God recompensed Job (Isaiah 40:2). He gave him a comeback - double for all his troubles (but same number of children). People thought it was over, but God came through. Whatever people have concluded about your life, to your disadvantage, God will turn it around for you today, in Jesus' Name. Beloved, that broken marriage shall experience a comeback again. That scattered family will be assembled together again. That dead business will yet bring you the joy of profiting. Your finances will spring back again, in Jesus' Name. Expect a comeback!

Here are seven daily suggestions for a permanent comeback:

1. **Pray, no matter how busy you are.** If you do, God promises to "direct you" (Proverbs 3:6). The difference between "drifting" and being "directed" is in acknowledging Him.

2. **Read His Word.** His Word produced new life in Sarah's dead womb, and calmed the storm in Galilee. Jesus told us we could not live by bread alone; we must have His word (Matthew 4:4). Don't leave the house until you read it.

3. **Tell your family that you love them.** If you feel awkward, read your Bible and see how often God says it to you (John 3:16), then take a leaf out of His book.

4. **Open yourself to new relationships.** God says, "I will bless thee…and thou shalt be a blessing" (Genesis 12:2). You are the carrier of somebody else's blessings. If you shut the door to blessings going out, you will also prevent blessings from coming in.

5. **Keep yourself in top shape.** When God needed someone to lead Saul of Tarsus to Christ, Ananias said, "I am here LORD" (Acts 9:10). Can you say that? Be ready and available (spiritually, physically, and emotionally) to God this day.

6. **Maintain a positive attitude.** Dominate your turf with faith. When the conversation turns negative, steer it back to, "whatever things are of good report" (Philippians 4:8).

7. **Worship and praise Him.** A common denominator in the life of those who are truly great, and from one generation to the other is the value they place on giving God His place in their lives in praise, worship and thanksgiving. The psalmist recognized this with what he said in Psalms 67:3-5.

Everybody needs a comeback, and Jesus is offering you a comeback today. No matter the obstacles, mistakes, or season, God's purpose and plan shall prevail. Let us pray it through.

## PRAYERS

1. I bless my Hero, my Champion, my Destiny Helper and Destiny Changer this morning. He is great, and He does miracles so great; there is no one like Him! Praise Him.

2. Father, Thank You for Total Restoration, for Commanding the Gates, and this new day of 'The Comeback.' Thank You for making me special to You.

3. Father, reverse every negative conclusion people have drawn about my life, especially with respect to the present challenges (name them) I am going through, in Jesus' Name.

4. Father, what is most difficult for man is very easy for you. Therefore, LORD, take over every impossible case of my life and turn it around for my joy, in Jesus' Name.

5. Father, by your power, let every 'dry bone' in my life come alive again.

6. Father, let your spirit of comfort and encouragement see me through every challenge I am going through.

7. Father, level every mountain, fill every valley and straighten every crooked place standing between me and my inheritance in you, in Jesus' Name.

8. Thank Him – 'Almighty Father, Thank You – I have nothing to give You but to Thank You, my LORD, Almighty Father, Thank You!"

# DAY 20

# THE FLOODGATES OF HEAVEN ARE OPENED UNTO YOU!

*"And Jacob awaked out of his sleep, and he said, surely the LORD is in this place; and I knew it not. And he was afraid, and said, how dreadful this place is! This is none other but the house of God, and this is the gate of heaven" (Genesis 28:16-17).*

Surely, if hell has gates (Psalms 24:7; Matthew 16:18), Heaven must have too. So, there is the Gate of Heaven. Today, the Floodgates of Heaven are opened unto you, in Jesus' mighty Name.

Three outlines:

1. What happens when the floodgates of Heaven open?
2. Example of people that had open heavens.
3. What must I do to keep the door perpetually opened?

**1. What Happens When The Floodgates Of Heavens Open?** Where is the gate of heaven? The gate of Heaven is the meeting point between the mortal and the immortal; the human and the divine; and between the natural and the supernatural. Anyone that the gate is opened to is initiated into the realm of the supernatural.

- That is where the dead hear the voice of the Son of God and live (John 5:25).

- That is where the law of resurrection terminates the law of death by the force of faith (John 11:25-26).

- It is the place of the 'Now Possibility' (John 11:22).

- It is where captivity turns around like a dream (Psalms 126:1-3).

- It is a place of turnaround breakthroughs.

- When the floodgates of heaven open struggles end, and tears are wiped away (Revelation 21:4).

- It is where God makes all things new (Revelation 21:5).

- It is where the stories of men are re-written, new chapters are opened to a man and men enter into 'above the next level' in their endeavors and adventures on the earth (Mark 2:10-12).

- It is place of special and creative miracles (Mark 8:22-25).

- It is where a man's life begins to command supernatural experiences, occurrences, and explanations on the earth (Genesis 26:12-14).

**2. Jesus Enjoyed the Floodgates of Heaven:**
*"While he yet spake, behold, a bright cloud overshadowed them: and behold a voice out of the cloud, which said, This is*

111

*My beloved Son, in Whom I am well pleased; hear ye Him"*
*(Matthew 17:5).*

Also, in Matthew 3:13-17, the results of these are the supernatural experiences that followed Jesus' lifestyles on the earth. Everything he spoke to heard and obeyed him. Nothing refused him; everything answered sweat less to him. Others are Moses, the widow of Zarephath, Solomon, Peter, and so on.

**3. What Must I Do to Command the Floodgates of Heaven to Open?** The forces that open the gate of heaven to a man include the following:

- Obey the Word of God. Commitment to, compliance with, and addiction to the word of God opens the gate of heaven to man (Deuteronomy 28:1; 12-13). This was the case of Peter in Luke 5:5; "Master, we have toiled all the night... nevertheless at Thy word I will let down the net." The Heaven's gate keepers honor, respect, and obey a man who is moving in the direction of the Word of God; the man who is word driven, word saturated and word connected.

- Tithing. Heaven's gatekeepers refuse, reject and resist any man who fails to pay his tithes. They ensure that the gate of heaven is totally locked against him no matter his religious rituals and rigors. A non-tither has attracted devourers to every area of his life (Malachi 3:10-12).

- Aggressive Praying & Righteousness. Jesus went to the transfiguration mountain to pray when the gate of heaven was opened to Him. Jesus was a prayer addict (Mark 1:35; Luke 6:12, 4:2,22,44). The praying man will stop sinning and a sinning man will stop praying. Hebrews 1:9, says, "Thou hast loved righteousness and hated iniquity; therefore God...hath anointed thee with oil of gladness above thy fellows".

That explains why the floodgates of heaven were perpetually opened to Jesus and why He commanded the support of the heaven's gate keepers throughout his sojourn on earth. If you are a man of the Word, a tither and a prayer addict that loves righteousness, you will access the opening of the floodgates of heaven and all your days of sojourn on this side of eternity.

## PRAYERS

1. Begin to thank Him for yet another day. Thank Him for He is a covenant keeping and merciful God.

2. Begin to plead the Blood of Jesus upon your life to atone for your errors and shortcomings.

3. Every act of violation and breaking of Scriptures in my life, blood of Jesus, forgive me, in Jesus' Name.

4. Thou floodgates of heaven, open unto me as from today by the Blood of the Lamb and by the mercy of God, in Jesus' Name.

5. I revoke and annul right now every evil law that is remotely controlling my experiences on the earth, in Jesus' Name.

6. Every diversion and perversion inflicted upon my destiny, be reversed now by fire, in Jesus' Name.

7. I command the anointing for the now possibility to rest upon my life as from today, in Jesus' Name.

8. Oh, thou my destiny, begin to experience new things; turnaround breakthroughs and promotions above the next level in every area of my life as from today, in Jesus' Name.

9. I command that as from today, life begins to answer, support, and favor and help me on every side, in Jesus' Name.

10. I decree that what had become hard for me in the past years shall become easy for me from today and beyond, in Jesus' Name.

11. Thank God for prayers answered.

# DAY 21

# 'OCCUPY TILL I COME'

*"And he called his ten servants, and delivered them ten pounds, and said unto them, occupy till I come" (Luke 19:13).*

Other translations say, "Do business till I come." In other words, engage in trade with what you have been given. Take what you have and put it to work. Stay busy with what I have given to you. Make this money grow. If you are in the church or business and you're not growing or going forward, you have become stagnant. Revelation 3:16 "So then, because you are lukewarm, and neither cold nor hot, 1 will spew you out of my mouth".

**To Occupy means:**

- To increase our evangelistic and missionary efforts by taking both the geographical and spiritual landscape for Jesus and making disciples of all nations.

- To summon courage to go after the enemy, and recover the kingdoms that once belonged to the church, like the cathedrals that have turned to bars.

- To accelerate and gain speed in the race or journey of life.

- To accomplish much within a short period of time; to subdue opposition, roadblocks, barriers, and break through into new lands.

- To overcome status quo and turn barriers into opportunities.

- To experience positive change of position, status, location, identity and destiny as the journey of life continues.

- To refuse to stay where you are, to push ahead to a higher ground of holiness and love for the community where you're desperately needed to show the love of Jesus.

Everyday must be a plus. Everyday, there is a positive change, a new experience, an exciting and fulfilling experience. My question is this: is the church really occupying, or are we just doing business as usual? There are great revivals in the world with hundreds of thousands and even millions giving their lives to Jesus Christ, but are we really occupying? How can we, as Christians, step across our own man-made lines and start acting as the body of Christ as a whole and not just a lot of parts? The barriers have to come down. How can we occupy if we cannot even come to agreement within ourselves? Jesus said a kingdom divided against itself cannot stand.

I believe we, as believers, have certainly inhabited the land but have not truly occupied it. To occupy is to fully influence every aspect of society as we know it, spiritually, as well as socially and economically. Society should see a dramatic change. This kind of change doesn't just affect a generation, but affects future generations as well.

If you change a culture, you change the very fabric of the society that they live in. This kind of change can have long lasting effects, not just temporary ones.

We can only make disciples of all nations by positively changing them from the inside out. Other religions have a systematic plan for doing just that. However, Christianity hasn't been doing that to some degree. All Christians are not called into the 5-fold ministry, but many are called to be bankers, teachers, lawyers, judges, politicians, and so on. Christians should be at the top and spread throughout every area of society if they are truly walking in their gifts.

There is an anointing that goes along with that calling. The God-given abilities, along with the anointing that is upon God's chosen people in every area of society, can influence that society in such a way as to give Godly direction and influence. This will produce a sustained change that will endure into the future, and I believe will be the catalyst that ushers in the second coming of the LORD Jesus Christ! Instead of sitting on our spiritual backsides, waiting for the LORD to return, let's hasten His return. Let's fill our lamps with oil and go take the land.

We all have our God-given places and it will take all of us working together in every phase of society to bring about the kind of permanent change that can transform a nation. We need Christians occupying every area of society. I want to personally challenge you to find your God-given place, and let's do this together. "Therefore, wake up from your slumber O thou that sleepeth; therefore, "give not sleep to thine eyes, nor slumber to thine eyelids" (Proverbs 6:4). The time to occupy (engage, take-back, stay relevant, evangelize, live holy and grow healthy) is NOW!

# PRAYERS

1. Thank God for another day. He is a prayer-answering God and a Covenant-keeping God. Begin to plead the Blood of Jesus upon your life for atonement, purging and redemption from all sins.

2. Father, teach me to know what to do with the seeds you have placed in my hands, in Jesus' Name. I will not eat up my seed, neither will I sow in the wrong land and wrong season, in Jesus' Name.

3. As I get my location right, help me to do the right things there, in Jesus' Name.

4. Every anti-change & anti-progress spirit that is monitoring my life and destiny, be roasted by fire, in Jesus' Name. Power for my next level, fall upon me right now, in Jesus' Name.

5. Oh thou my destiny, continue to ascend the ladder of life from today and don't stop until Jesus comes.

6. I command the spirit of "Esek" (contention) and the spirit of "Sitnah" (opposition) assigned against my inheritance to die by fire, in Jesus' name (Genesis 26:20-22).

7. Oh God, release fresh oil for the next level upon my life everyday as from today, in Jesus' Name.

# DAY 22

# DISTINCTIONS

*"Then were the king's scribes called at that time in the third month, that is, the month Sivan, on the three and twentieth day thereof; and it was written according to all that Mordecai commanded unto the Jews, and to the lieutenants, and the deputies and rulers of the provinces which are from India unto Ethiopia, an hundred twenty and seven provinces, unto every province according to the writing thereof, and unto every people after their language, and to the Jews according to their writing, and according to their language" (Esther 8:9).*

We bless the name of the LORD for bringing us through the past few days when the floodgates of Heaven were opened, and when the LORD gave us double promotion, favor and anointing. Today, the LORD said, has been set aside for those who are called by His name to be treated with special honor, attention, and to favor a people of distinctions.

The third month in the Jewish calendar is called 'Sevan'. It was mentioned in the book of Esther (Esther 8:9). It was on this day that the Jew-hater, Haman, was hanged in gallows he prepared for Mordecai. Mordecai was then given the ring of authority, and the house of Haman was turned over to Esther. Then the Jews were granted permission to "...stand for their life, to destroy, to slay, cause to perish anyone that would assault them...take the spoil of them for a prey" (Esther 8:11). It is also in this month that God decided to set his people apart as a kingdom of priests and a holy nation (Exodus 19:6-8). Power is given to you this day to enter into the enemies' warehouse and take back all he has stolen from you, in Jesus' Name.

Also, remember that it was in the month of Sivan, my (our) LORD and Master, the Lion of the tribe of Judah, rose triumphantly from the grave; "having spoiled principalities and powers, He made a shew of them openly, triumphing over them in it" (Colossians 2:15). Jesus said unto her, "I am the Resurrection, and the Life: he that believeth in me, though he were dead, yet shall he live" (John 11:25). It is the month of the Resurrection/Easter, an event that assures us of our hope for eternity with God. It is your season of decoration, when your light will shine, in Jesus Name.

I am here to announce to you that all these events that happened were not an accident. Jesus could have been killed and resurrected any other month except the month in which it occured. However, according to the divine calendar, there are some liberties, benefits, rights and privileges that can only be enjoyed in the month of Sivan. He makes a way where there seems to be no way. The month of Sivan was when the tomb was sealed up, yet the moment the power of resurrection descended, a way was made. I decree into your life: every way/ road that has been closed to you shall be opened by the resurrection power, in Jesus' Name.

The resurrection power brings justice to the Jews in the days of Esther. Also, the evil one thought he had prevailed over 'The Truth'; that perhaps they had killed and buried 'The Truth". Indeed, sometimes, the wicked prosper in their wickedness, but when the Power of resurrection shows up, they are exposed and disgraced. The LORD shall liberate you today. Every lie against you shall be exposed, and the liar disgraced, in Jesus' Name.

The resurrection power reactivates life. In the case of Lazarus, a decaying body came alive and anew (John 11:44). I decree into your life that whatever has seen decay and corruption in your life by the activities of the wicked, the LORD shall reactivate to life, in Jesus' Name. The decayed season shall be resurrected, in Jesus Name.

Where you have been struggling to rise, the power of resurrection will lift you up, in Jesus' Name. Every power that has paralyzed your life, business, or marriage shall be destroyed today, in Jesus' Name. No one was able to keep Jesus down. From now on, you will become difficult to hinder, impossible to be silenced, and unable to be buried in Jesus' Name.

The trumpet has sounded in heaven for your coming forth, to be recognized, made distinct, and decorated. So, what are you waiting for? Isaiah 60:1 says, "arise and shine… the glory of the LORD is risen upon you."

What are your responsibilities? The American Constitution, unlike the Bible, has one basic flaw. "It clearly delineates the Bill of Rights, but it nowhere states a Bill of Responsibilities...Our American government ensures people their rights but fails to clearly spell out their responsibilities, fails to call them to be the kind of people God wants them to be."

### God wants you to:

- Run from Sin like a plague. "Thou hast loved righteousness and hated iniquity..." (Hebrews 1:9)

- Pray and fast. "Elijah was a man (not an angel) subject to like passions as we are, and he prayed earnestly..." (James 5:17)

-  Fulfill your financial obligation to your church and family (Luke 6:38).

- Go out of your way to tell somebody that Jesus loves them, or go and help somebody with a random act of kindness (Matthew 25:45).

## PRAYERS

1. Every time I see another breaking of the day, I say Thank You LORD. Thank Him, bless Him, glorify the Covenant-keeping God.

2. Thank Him for making you see another day, week and month. It's not a right but a privilege (Lamentations 3:21-23).

3. Plead the Blood of Jesus on your soul, family and church for forgiveness, cleansing and restoration (1 John 1:8).

4. Father, let me experience the power of resurrection in

a new way, in Jesus' Name.

5. Father, make me a man/woman of distinction; every test, every recognition, and every award shall be with distinctions, in Jesus' Name.

6. Father, let life be given to every organ (be specific) in my body that is experiencing decay, in Jesus' Name.

7. Father, let every stone rolled against me and my loved ones by those that hate me be rolled back at them today, in Jesus' Name (John 11:39).

8. Father, don't let me offend you; keep me pure and holy (1 Chronicles 4:10), in Jesus' Name.

# DAY 23

# DIVINE PERFORMANCE

*"Now therefore give me this mountain, whereof the LORD spake in that day…if so be the LORD will be with me, then I shall be able to drive them out, as the LORD said. 13. And Joshua blessed him, and gave unto Caleb… Hebron therefore became the inheritance of Caleb…because that he wholly followed the LORD God of Israel" (Joshua 14:12-14).*

Our God is Omniscient, Omnipotent, All-knowing and All- Sufficient. The One that has no equal, no comparison and distinctively great says He has a plan for you. All that He has promised you shall find fulfillment, in Jesus' Name.

God knows your challenges; unkept promises by man, the disappointments and heartaches. However, like Esther, you're marching into your appointed throne and palace (Esther 2:16), in Jesus' Name. The water of calamities trying to swallow and drown you into oblivion has receded and you will see the top of the mountains of joy, breakthrough and laughter, in Jesus' Name (Genesis 8:5).

Naturally in life, there is a gap between prophecies or promises, and fulfillment, performance or manifestation. God's will is that this gap be as short as possible. He always desires to hasten His word for performance (Jeremiah 1:12).

Satan always desires to delay, elongate or even stop the fulfillment of prophecy. In the life of Abraham and Sarah, there was a gap of about 25 years in the performance of the prophecy of the birth of Isaac (laughter). For Israel's deliverance from bondage, it was thirty years. In the life of Caleb, it was 45 years (Joshua 14:5-14). For many people, prophecies never translate into fulfillment until they die. That would not be your portion, in Jesus' Name.

Therefore, for prophecies to give birth to performance, a great deal of force must be exerted by the recipient of the prophecy.

**Force of Prayer:** Prayer is the vital force that ultimately activates prophecies for performance as seen in Jeremiah 29:12-14. If Caleb had not demanded for Hebron after 45 years of the promise, he probably would have lost it forever and denied the tribe of Judah their rightful inheritance of that chosen land in Canaan. He that asketh receiveth (Matthew 7:8, Luke 18:1).

**Force of Obedience & Holiness:** Joshua 14:14, "... because that he wholly followed the LORD God of Israel."

If you are willing and obedient, you will eat the good (best) of the land (Isaiah 1:18; Hebrews 12:14).

**Force of God's Word:** Fill your heart with God's Word more and more (Ephesians 3:16; Psalms 18:44).

*"...as you have spoken in mine ears, so will I do unto you."*
*Numbers 14:28,*

**Force of Fasting and Service:** Fast more (Matthew 17:21), and serve God more (Hebrew 6:10).

I decree that all long-awaited prophecies and delayed blessings shall be expedited for performance as we pray, in Jesus' Name!

## PRAYERS

1. Father, Thank You for a new day. You're a Covenant keeping God. Thank You for preserving me and my family thus far. "The steadfast love of the LORD never ceases, they are new every morning, and great is your faithfulness..." (Lamentations 3:23).

2. Father, forgive me of all my sins by the power of your shed blood and clothe me with a new garment of righteousness, in Jesus' Name.

3. As I grow in age, keep me strong, both spiritually and physically, to be able to run with the vision of my life, in Jesus' Name.

4. Father, let every obstacle placed on the route to my destiny become a divine accelerator to the fulfillment of my dreams and visions, in Jesus' Name.

5. Father, incapacitate any man or spirit that is standing in opposition to the fulfillment of your good thoughts, plans and prophecies for my life, in Jesus' Name.

6. Every power that is assigned to elongate the battles and afflictions of my life be devoured now by fire, in Jesus' Name.

7. Begin to declare and enforce right now whatever you know that God has spoken about you and the circumstances of your life.

# DAY 24

# DIVINE SETTLEMENT

*"But may the God of all grace, who called us to His eternal glory by Christ Jesus, after you have suffered a while, perfect, establish, strengthen, and SETTLE you" (1 Peter 5:10).*

Once again, we bless our LORD and Master for another new day. This day, the LORD promised to settle all those whose names are in the book of life.

My prayer for you today is divine settlement. The time has come when God will settle you in every area of your life. In your finances, your health, your marriage, in all your relationships, and your family. For the singles, He will settle you in your homes. He will establish and settle your business. God will establish and settle you at the top and in high places. God will settle your case in every area where the enemy has fought against you, in Jesus' Name! The Dictionary defines settlement as 'an act of fixing or steadying'; 'a deal or a bargain between two or more parties'; Better still 'it is when one or something is taken out of discomfort to a comfortable place' (Exodus 3:7-8).

It is to 'Fix' something or someone.'

Just like the roller coasters in Disney World, Kenny Wood and other fun centers of the world throw us up and down, Life is also a journey of ups and downs, valley experiences and mountaintop experiences, etc. The beautiful thing is that the Sovereign God ensures no condition is permanent. "Though weeping may tarry for the night, joy surely will surface in the morning" (Psalms 30:5). The season for your settlement and steadily moving into your comfort zone has come.

However, divine settlement only comes after we have faced and overcome our suffering and passed. The road of life without challenges along its path probably leads to nowhere significant. Human suffering, hardship or challenges could serve as veritable stepping stones to greatness. In Genesis 32:22-28, we read how God settled Jacob. His challenges were numerous, and every step of the way, we find his brother's settlement, Uncle's settlement, Papa's settlement, satanic settlement, and ultimately God's settlement. Jacob ran away from Esau because of his (Esau's) murderous intention on a business deal that one thought he was taken advantage of, even though the contract was legitimate.

1. Esau's settlement started with an intention to kill and destroy his brother, then coming with 400 dagger-drawn soldiers to settle 20 years of robbery, so they can resolve the quarrel once and for all. Finally, Genesis 33:9 reads, "I have enough, my brother; keep that thou hast unto thine self."

2. Uncle Laban's settlement: After Jacob had served him for twenty years, see how Laban settled Jacob: Genesis

31:41, "Thus have I been twenty years in thy house, I served thee fourteen years for thy two daughters, and six years for thy cattle, and thou has changed my wages ten times (downward)." If not for the divine warning, he planned to take Jacob back to captivity and servitude without reward. Genesis 31:24, "and God came to Laban the Syrian in a dream by night, and said to him, take heed that thou speak not to Jacob good or bad."

3. Papa Isaac's Settlement: It got him four wives, 12 children, "plenty of oxen, asses, flocks, menservants and women servants" (Genesis 32:5).

4. Satanic Settlement: John 10:10a says, "… to steal, kill and destroy." First from Esau, then Laban and eventually the 400 dagger-drawn soldiers of Esau could have finished in less than 20 minutes what he got for twenty years.

5. God's settlement: The covenant keeping God settled Jacob by making him a Nation, Israel, and blessed him beyond his wildest imagination. The disciples came to Jesus and asked, "how will you settle us too?" (Mark 10:30) "But ye shall receive an hundredfold now in this time, houses and brethren, sisters, brothers, children, lands, with persecutions, and in the world to come eternal life."

We often see great people and admire or envy their status and positions, but we rarely venture to hear their stories. There is a story behind every glory we see. Apostle Paul said in 1 Timothy 2:12 that "if we suffer with Christ, we shall reign with him." In other words, it is only those who have suffered with Christ that are qualified to reign with

Him.

The days of your mourning are over; it's your time to be settled. Are you going through any suffering now in your journey? Don't despair, don't give up, don't quit. Remember, the suffering of the moment can never be compared to the glory which always lies ahead of every true suffering handled in a Godly way.

Brethren, settlement comes into play when two parties agree (Amos 3:3). Jacob was settled because he agreed with the angel of the LORD (Christophany). It was an appearance of Jesus Christ in the Old Testament because only Jesus can change a man's name, not an angel (Genesis. 32: 28). People of God, if you want your issue(s) to be settled, the following points are your "Bill of Responsibilities":

- You must give your life to and acknowledge The LORD Jesus Christ as your personal Savior (John 3:16).

- You must call or cry out for help (Matthew 7:7-8; Mark 10: 46-48).

- You must fulfill your financial obligation to your church and family (1 Timothy 5:8; Malachi 3:10).

- Give God Radical Praise & Worship (Acts 16:25).

- Follow peace with all men and holiness (Hebrews 12:14).

# PRAYERS

1. Father, I praise and thank You for a new day. I thank You for commanding the light of your glory upon my destiny. Bless the Covenant-making and Covenant-keeping God.

2. Holy Ghost, bring an end to 'unprofitable' labor in my life, in Jesus' Name. Let my hands be hands that profit, eyes that see the invisible, ears that hear the inaudible, hands that heal the sick and perform miracles, and feet that are planted on the Rock, in Jesus' Name.

3. O LORD, please, settle me today: In my finances, in my health, my marriage, and in all my relationships and my family. Settle me O LORD!

4. Father, just as Saul got tired of pursuing the life of David and he slept off, put divine tiredness on all that pursue after my divine settlement in life. Let them go into sleep, in Jesus' Name.

5. (Hold your head as you take this next prayer point). Father, my head rejects the influence of the rod of wickedness on my life. You rod of wickedness sent in my direction, catch fire now and burn down to ashes, in Jesus' Name

6. Please LORD, don't let me offend you. Keep me in the straight and the narrow way. Let me hunger and thirst for your word daily, in Jesus Name.

7. Thank You, LORD, for prayers answered.

# DAY 25

# FINISHING STRONG

*"Thou crownest the year with thy goodness; and thy paths drop fatness" (Psalms 65:11).*

The race of life is a marathon and not a sprint; it is a long-distance race that requires courage, stamina, and discipline. Similarly, our journey through the calendar year is also a marathon and not a sprint. A journey of 365 days; 52 weeks; 12 months; 7 days; 8,760 hours; 525,600 minutes, and 31,536,000 seconds. It's not a joke at all.

Survival through the year is not a joke at all. It is a big deal that you and I are alive today. Life is a battle; a journey of oppositions and confrontations. You are destined in life to finish well and in victory, but it's not automatic. You need to fight with the right mentality, faith in God, help from God and a godly strategy to win well.

Many started life badly, but they ended well and many started well and ended well. The examples of bad starters are numerous in the Bible. The likes of Jabez (1 Chronicles

4:9-10), blind Bartimaeus (Mark 10:49-50), and the thief on the cross (Luke 23:39-43), started badly but, somehow, by the grace of God, they finished well and strong. You might have started badly and are still wondering how it's going to end. Wonder no more. I have good news for you today; God will pull through for you. God is about to pull you out of the jaw of defeat to give you an overwhelming victory. "It doesn't matter where you have been; it only matters where you're going" - Brian Tracy. Listen, "...the race is not for the swift, nor the battle to the strong, neither yet bread to the wise, nor yet riches to men of understanding, nor yet favor to them of skill, but time and chance happeneth to them all" (Ecclesiastes 9:11). It is your time and season!

Many started well and continued well and finished well. The likes of Isaac who had a good start, prospered, and went forward. In Genesis 26:12-14, the Bible says, "Then Isaac sowed in that land, and received in the same year an hundredfold: and the LORD blessed him. And the man waxed great, and went forward, and grew until he became very great: For he had possession of flocks, and possession of herds, and great store of servants: and the Philistines envied him".

Our LORD and Master, Jesus Christ of Nazareth had a good start. "He waxed strong in the Spirit as a child, filled with wisdom" (Luke 2:40). The Bible says the grace of God was upon Him. In Luke 2:52, the Bible says, "He increased in wisdom, stature, and favor with man and God." At the Cross, He said, "I have glorified thee on earth: I have finished the work which thou gavest me to do" (John 17:4). Like Jesus, you will finish well and strong, in Jesus' Name.

Hear His Promises, "Thou crownest the year with thy goodness; and thy paths drop fatness" (Psalms 65:11). God will crown all your efforts of the past with goodness, excellence and the best of everything, in Jesus' Name. The remaining days of your life shall be the best ever for you, in Jesus' Name. Until you prevail in praying and pray through, your purpose, mandate, commission and assignment on earth remains a mirage. Prayer will bring creations on the path of destiny fulfillment. For the accomplishment of life to be easy for you, for you to accomplish purpose and fulfill destiny, you need to pray hard, pray well and pray through.

*"It is not where you start, it's where you finish that counts."*
—*Zig Ziglar.*

Always chose to finish well and strong. It's up to you now!

## PRAYERS

1. Begin to thank God for today. Thank Him for securing the months, weeks and days ahead of you with pleasantness, peace, prosperity and joy.

2. Begin to plead the Blood of Jesus upon your life for cleansing and sanctification.

3. Every power that is frustrating my efforts and moves that I make in life, resisting my desires and pursuits from generating a commensurate result, be consumed by fire, IN JESUS' NAME.

4. Father, please crown the remaining part of my life with success and let my path flow with favor, goodness and fatness of the earth, in Jesus' Name.

5. I prophesy to every aspect of my life and destiny, you shall accomplish purpose, fulfill destiny and see the goodness of the LORD in the land of the living from today, in Jesus' Name.

6. Thou grounds of my destiny, begin to yield your increase unto me, in Jesus' Name.

7. Father, let my altar of prayer, study, and worship constantly burn with fire, in Jesus' Name.

8. Power to work straight, talk straight, hear straight, see straight and do that which is right in the sight of the LORD, I receive, in Jesus' Name.

9. Begin to thank God for prayers answered.

# DAY 26

# SUCCESSFUL ACCOMPLISHMENTS

*"Solomon successfully accomplished all that came into his heart to make in the house of the LORD and in his own house"* *(2 Chronicles 7:11).*

Welcome to another day that the LORD has made. The LORD has been faithful in giving us something memorable to remember daily. The God of David and Solomon is even promising a great finishing for you today. Hear what He did for Solomon regarding God's project, and his personal project in 2 Chronicles 7:11, "Solomon successfully accomplished all that came into his heart to make in the house of the LORD and in his own house." That will be your story & testimony, in Jesus' Mighty Name.

## BIBLICAL BASIS

1.  "I sent you to reap whereon ye bestowed no labor; other men labored, and ye are entered into their labors" (John

4:38).

2.  Laboring and harvesting are two distinct things; not everyone who labors receives a commensurate harvest.

3.  There are three categories of people here:

    -   Those who labor and never enter their harvest.

    -   Those who labor and get some or all their harvest.

    -   Those who access the harvest of others, regardless of whether they labored for it or not.

    *"Thou crownest the year with thy goodness; and thy paths drop fatness" Psalms 65:11*

    The race of life is a marathon and not a sprint; it is a long-distance race that requires courage and stamina. Similarly, our journey through the calendar year is also a marathon, not a sprint; a journey of 365 days, 52 weeks, 12 months, 8760 hours. It is a big deal that you and I are alive today.

4.  Matthew 20:6-8 says, "…And about the eleventh hour, he went out and found others standing idle, and said to them, 'Why have you been standing here idle all day?' They said to him, 'Because no one hired us.' He said to them, 'You also go into the vineyard, and whatever is right you will receive. "So when evening had come, the owner of the vineyard said to his steward, 'Call the laborers and give them their wages, beginning with the last to the first."

Result is not based on performance but GRACE! Activity does not equate achievement.

# 4 ESSENTIAL RESPONSIBILITIES FOR SUCCESSFUL ACCOMPLISHMENTS

Looking at Apostle Paul, (2 Timothy 4:6-8) and other good finishers, I have concluded that there are four fundamental actions we can take to help us finish well (add yours):

1.  A Daily Time of Focused Personal Communion with God: Practicing the Presence of God is an excellent habit to cultivate. But the foundation of that has to be a time of focused personal communion with God, and it needs to be daily. "Demas, in love with this present world, has deserted me and gone to Thessalonica" (2 Timothy 4:10). Demas didn't just wake up one day and make a 90-degree turn. That doesn't happen. Demas drifted little by little towards the attractions of the world. And if you and I do not practice this daily focused time of communion with God, we will find ourselves also drifting in the wrong direction.

2.  A Daily Commitment to God as A Living Sacrifice: Romans 12:1 says, "I appeal to you therefore, brothers, by the mercies of God, to present your bodies as a living sacrifice, holy and acceptable to God, which is your spiritual worship." As we daily reflect on the gospel and what God has done for us in Christ, this should lead us to present ourselves as daily, living sacrifices. Why? 1 Corinthians 6:19-20 says, "You are not your own, for you were bought with a price…" For some, it might mean reducing one's standard of living in order to be able to give more to God's kingdom

work. For some, it means being willing to continually give our self to the ministry God has given us. It may also mean 'not feeling sorry for myself' and willfully telling God, I accept the challenges of ministry from you, and Thank You for the privilege of being in your ministry.

3. A firm belief in the sovereignty and love of God: 'Life is difficult.' Most people would agree with that. If you've lived very long, you'll realize life is difficult, or at least it's often difficult, and sometimes it's even painful. And over time, you will experience both difficulties and pain. So, if you want to endure to the end, if you want to stand firm in the face of life's difficulties and pain, then you must have a firm belief in the sovereignty and the love of God.

You must not only believe that God is in control of every event in His universe and specifically, every event in your own life, but that God, in exercising that control, He does so from His infinite love for you. It's possible that sometime in your life, things will totally fall apart and you will feel that you have nothing left. Let me tell you, there are two things that God will never take away: God will never take away the Gospel. Second, God will never take away His promises.

4. Persevere in Prayer with Thanksgiving: Therefore, dear soldier in the LORD's army, we are to persevere by standing firm in the place of prayer. We move forward in thanksgiving. When Paul says, "I have finished the race" (2 Timothy 4:7), obviously, he was talking about motion. And perseverance means to keep going in spite of obstacles. So when Paul says, "I have finished the

140

race," he was saying, "I have persevered in the place of prayer". We must move forward in faith and begin to acknowledge Him in thanksgiving for what He has done, is doing and still will do. We must be like Paul and say, "I have fought the good fight, I have finished the race, I have kept the faith." That will be your testimony today, in Jesus' Name.

Yes, they are the essentials. However, standing over all of them is the grace of God. The same apostle who said, "I have fought the good fight, I have finished the race, I have kept the faith," also said in another context, "But by the grace of God I am what I am" (1 Corinthians 15:10). Paul attributed all of his endurance, all of his faithfulness, to the grace of God. And so, as we look at our responsibility, keep in mind that we are enabled to fulfill that responsibility only by the grace of God. May you and I be like the apostle Paul, in Jesus' Name.

## PRAYERS

1. My father, my father, Thank You for your goodness unto me and my family today. Thank You because I know that my remaining days shall be glorious; I will finish well, and accomplish all that you've purposed for me, in Jesus' Name.

2. My father, my father, I receive grace to run well today, in Jesus' Name. One thing that I know, and I know for sure, if we follow God strong enough, the things that we are following after are the ones that will begin to follow us. That is the place of right priorities (Matthew 6:33).

3. My father, my father, let every goal that I have been

pursuing be the ones pursuing me from today, in the Name of Jesus.

4. My father, my father, any power or forces that do not want me to do well, will not prosper in my life in Jesus name. Jeremiah 22:30; "This is what the LORD says" "Let the record show that this man Jehoiachin was childless; He is a failure, for none of his children will succeed him on the throne of David to rule over Judah" shall be the portion of our enemies, in Jesus' Name.

5. Colossians 2:14 says, "Blotting out the handwriting of ordinances that was against us…" My father, my father, every evil handwriting working against my glory, against my breakthrough, against my success, you will not prosper. By the power in the blood of the lamb, I cancel them, in the Name of Jesus.

6. Father, frustrate every plan to separate me from my harvest, and link me up with the unclaimed harvests of those who have gone ahead of me in my family and field of labor.

7. Thank You, LORD, for prayers answered.

## DAY 27

# HEAVEN BY REVELATION

*"And the building of the wall of it was of jasper: and the city was pure gold, like unto clear glass. And the foundations of the wall of the city were garnished with all manner of precious stones. The first foundation was jasper; the second, sapphire; the third, a chalcedony; the fourth, an emerald; The fifth, sardonyx; the sixth, sardius; the seventh, chrysolyte; the eighth, beryl; the ninth, a topaz; the tenth, a chrysoprasus; the eleventh, a jacinth; the twelfth, an amethyst. And the twelve gates were twelve pearls: every several gate was of one pearl: and the street of the city was pure gold, as it were transparent glass"* (Revelation 21:18-21).

My prayer is that we all experience the blessing of God that cannot be denied in the new day, in Jesus' Name (Amen). Two days back, we considered Finishing Strong; yesterday, it was Successful Accomplishment. Today, the theme is Heaven by Revelation.

Our generation is beginning to forget about Heaven; we don't preach, talk or pray about it anymore, it seems. In this fast-paced world, we have placed Heaven on the shelf as though it's merely a vacation spot. Beloved, I am here to remind you that we need to get back to believing in the reality of Heaven. Sir/Ma, if you can simply get a glimpse of the glory and beauty of Beulah land, then, no pain will be too much, no insult too big simply to make it there; no glitter or gold in this world can erase the memory.

An American tourist visited the 19th century Polish rabbi, Chofetz Chaim. He was astonished to see that the rabbi's home was but a simple room filled with books, plus a table and a bench. He asked the rabbi where his furniture was. The rabbi asked the tourist why he did not have any furniture either. The tourist asserted that he was but a visitor. To this, Chofetz Chaim responded that he was also only a visitor passing through, hence the sparseness of furniture in his home. Jim Reeves, the songwriter and singer of blessed memory sang the song:

*"This world is not my home I'm just a-passing through My treasures are laid up somewhere beyond the blue; The angels beckon me from heaven's open door And I can't feel at home in this world anymore "*

Conversely, instead of being a people uncomfortable in a foreign land, often it seems that we have driven our stakes into the temporal soil of this world. We do not appear to hold the same urgency that our forefathers had, anticipating His coming at any moment. It is time that we turn our hearts toward Heaven and take responsibility for getting souls there.

Before I get ahead of myself, some terms will be quickly defined: Heaven: God said, "Heaven is My throne and the earth is My footstool" (Isaiah 66:1). Jesus said, "In my Father's house are many mansions" (John 14:2). Not apartments, studios or houses; He called them mansions. The Celestial shores beckon us each day. You can miss everything, but please don't miss heaven. Heaven is a place of intimacy, beauty and adventure. Unfortunately, people don't get excited about heaven anymore. Please understand that there are 3 Heavens made known to us in the Holy Bible. They are the atmosphere above the earth where birds and airplanes fly; the firmament of Heaven that the stars and planetary systems occupy; and the Heaven of Heavens, which is the "Dwelling Place of God."

# REVELATION

Revelation means making something secret or hidden known (Oxford Advanced Learner's Dictionary, Special Price Edition). Deuteronomy 29:29 says, "The secret things belong unto the LORD our God: but those things which are revealed belong unto us and to our children forever, that we may do all the words of this law."

Heaven by Revelation, therefore, implies that unless you get the realities of heaven by divine revelation, you may never love, desire or pray for it. The Apostles had a revelation of Heaven; many were burnt at the stakes, crucified upside down, fed to lions and even beheaded. Yet, the revelation of Heaven made their suffering nothing, compared to the joy that awaits them in the Heavenly Jerusalem. Classic examples are Stephen (Acts 7:55-56; 60), Apostle Paul (Acts 20:22-24), & John the Beloved (Revelation 21:18-20).

Time and space will not allow me to talk about the intimacy, adventure, party, and beauty of Heaven. I will take a small jab at its beauty, though, to give us an idea what we're talking about. Intimacy, relationship filled to overflowing, is not enough to satisfy us as humans; there is another ache from deep within – our longing for beauty. A few months ago, my family and I were in Orlando, Florida, for a family vacation. On one of our nights there, I decided to go sight- seeing at the Waldorf Astoria in Orlando, Florida. It was a wowing experience – the beautifully manicured lawns, the carpet on the floor, sounds of music and laughter, the scent of the flower beds in the warm ocean breeze. I saw beauty, yet a voice within me said, "This is not home, heaven is more beautiful. This is like a comparison between a miniature golf course and a real championship course; there is no comparison whatsoever."

As humans, we long for beauty. C.S. Lewis said, "One of the mistakes we so often make when captured by an object of beauty, whether it's a place, a person, or a work of art, is to assume that the longing in our heart is for the thing before us". These things are but shadows of the realities to come.

- The beauty of the tabernacle carried by Israel through the desert was a type of the real item in heaven. However, no matter the hormone treatment, a cat can never be a lion. So, it goes with all things on earth; the beauty that so captures our heart and is so fleeting draws us toward the eternal reality.

- When the biblical writers speak of heaven, they use the most beautiful imagery they can. "In the midst of the street of it, and on either side of the river, was there the tree of life, which bare twelve manner of fruits, and yielded her fruit every month: and the leaves of the tree were for the healing of the nations" (Revelations 22:2).

• Also, we have Heaven's New Jerusalem, an unspeakable beauty, a city with streets of gold, gates of pearl, and precious stones (Revelations 21:10-21; read Revelations 21-22). "And the city had no need of the sun, neither of the moon to shine in it: for the glory of God did lighten it, and the Lamb is the light thereof" (Revelations 21:23).

• A Christian's eternal inheritance – "To an inheritance incorruptible and undefiled, and that fadeth not away, re- served in heaven for you" (1 Peter 1:4)

When you die, do you want to go there? Every sane human being will desire to go to Heaven. The alternative to not going to Heaven is going to hell, where the devil and his demons hold sway. Everyone who ends up in hell has eternity to regret his or her folly while here on earth, for rejecting Christ as personal LORD and Savior. "Then death and hades were cast into the lake of fire. This is the second death. And anyone not found written in the Book of Life was cast into the lake of fire" (Revelations 20:14-15). "Do you know that the unrighteous will not inherit the Kingdom of God? Do not be deceived, neither fornicators, nor idolaters, nor adulterers, nor homosexuals, nor sodomites, nor thieves, nor covetous, nor drunkards, nor revilers, nor extortioners, will inherit the kingdom of God" (1 Corinthians 6:9-10).

Board members, if you aren't trying to get someone to heaven, we don't need you on our board. Sunday School Teachers, if you aren't trying to get someone to heaven, we don't need you to teach Sunday school. Pastors and Prayer Warriors, stand; If you aren't trying to get your group to heaven, then we don't need you as a pastor or a member of the Praying Army. The job of the church is to get everyone ready for Heaven. Paul said, "Oh, that I might know Him, and the power of his resurrection" (Philippians 3:10). Let's sing: Oh, I want to see him, look upon His face...

# PRAYERS

1.  Worship the Creator of the Heaven and the Earth. Bless Jehovah El-Shaddai; The LORD of LORD, King of kings, Monarch of the Universe. Daniel 4:3 says, "How great are His signs, and how mighty are His wonders! His kingdom is an everlasting kingdom, and His dominion is from generation to generation."

2.  "Surely the LORD GOD will do nothing, but He revealeth His secret unto His servants, the prophets" (Amos 3:7) – Father, baptize me with revelation gifts, in Jesus' Name!

3.  Isaiah 1:11-16. God's demand for purity from His children is unchanging. "An unholy person pollutes every- thing that he touches with his impurity." Father, sanctify me holy. Create in me a clean heart, O LORD, and renew a right spirit within me" (Psalms 51:10).

4.  Father, create in me a thirst and hunger for the return of the LORD Jesus; a deep longing for a fresh revelation

of the soon-coming King. Help me to place an intimate relationship with you above making requests of you, in Jesus' Name!

5. Deliver me, O LORD, from a cold, calculating obedience.

6. I know a servant can serve without love; Father, make me a lover of God and the things of God. I give myself away, so I can love you more.

7. As I walk with You, O LORD, on a daily basis, may I receive the testimony from man and God like Enoch, "HE PLEASED GOD" Hebrews 11:5.

8. Thank You, LORD, for prayers answered. MARANATHA!

## DAY 28

# PREPARE FOR JOY

*"...beauty for ashes, the oil of joy for mourning, the garment of praise for the spirit of heaviness; that they might be called trees of righteousness, the planting of the LORD, that He might be glorified" (Isaiah 61:3).*

Today, God is saying "in spite of what you hear or what is going on, prepare for joy". I am talking about the Joy of the LORD, Joy in the LORD, and Joy that abideth forever more. God has heard your supplications and now, it's God's time to move on your behalf; so, put on your dancing shoes. God is about to have an appointment with those who are mourning in Zion, to give them, "...beauty for ashes, the oil of joy for mourning, the garment of praise for the spirit of heaviness; that they might be called trees of righteousness, the planting of the LORD, that He might be glorified" (Isaiah 61:3).

## World News: "Breaking News of Sorrow"

The news reports which we read and view on TV most times rarely bring joy. What we hear and view is news of murder, crime, recession, drop in profits, layoffs, job cuts. Breaking news is always about the terrorists and jihadists conquering and butchering their way across Iraq and Syria. Planes falling out of the sky on a weekly basis. Civilians being killed in massive numbers in the Israel-Gaza conflict. People dying of sickness and poverty; in short, it's like the world is falling apart!

## Fact or Truth: Preliminary Analysis

The world's news is full of sorrow - facts. Conversely, the gospel news is full of joy – truth. What drives your life, facts or truth? A review of the following passages communicates the counsel of the LORD concerning those who diligently seek Him: Psalms 37:25; Psalms 34:10; 17, 19; Psalms 27:1-3; and Psalms 23.

• Jesus Is the Source of Joy. Psalms 30:5; Luke 2:10-11; Matthew 2:10; Psalms 16:11; 1 Peter 1:8.

• The question is, "Can joy come in the midst of a recession?" The answer is, of course, a resounding YES! Why Is Jesus Able to Give Joy in A Recession?

• He is the Almighty - Exodus 15:3; Psalms 24:7-10; Psalms 91:1; Jeremiah 32:27; Jeremiah 32:17.

• He is the sure Help - Psalms 60:11, Psalms 124:8, Psalms 121:1-2, Psalms 46:1, Psalms 124:2-3.

• He is a Miracle Worker - Mark 5:34; John 5:8; Luke 7:13-14; Mark 5:41; John 11:43.

• His Name is above all other names - John 4:10, John 6:35, John 10:11, John 10:7, John 8:12, John 1:4-5, John 11:25, John 14:6; Isaiah 9:6; Revelation 1:8; Philippians 2:9.

- He is faithful - 1 Corinthians 10:13; Hebrews 10:23, Hebrews 11:11; Psalms 36:5; Lamentations 3:23; Numbers 23:19; Psalms 33:9.

## Biblical Sampling of Those Who Enjoyed Joy in Recession

- Isaac – Genesis 26:12-14.

- Israelites in Goshen experienced no hail, while hail plagued all the rest of Egypt – Exodus 9:26.

- Elijah was fed by ravens during the famine – 1 Kings 17:1-6.

- The Widow of Zarephath was fed by Elijah during the famine – 1 Kings 17:9-16.

- Rahab the Harlot – Joshua 6:20-25.

How did that happen? Are there things I need to do?

There is a preparation for joy.

## Preparing for Joy: Seven Guidelines

1. Abstain from sin - 1 Thessalonians 5:22; 4:3; 1 Peter 2:11.

2. Sign a deal with God - Joshua 2:12-14; 1 Samuel 1:11.

3. Key into God's program - Joshua 2:9; Hebrews 10:36.

4. Remain/dwell in His Presence - Psalms 16:11; 91:1-3.

5. Have faith in God - Hebrews 11:31.

6. Ask until your joy is full - John 16:24; Joshua 14:12-14.

7. Be wise in your request - Joshua 2:12-13; Ecclesiastes 5:2.

# PRAYERS

1.  Bless HIM: "I will love thee, O LORD, my strength. The LORD is my rock, and my fortress, and my deliverer; my God, my strength, in whom I will trust; my buckler, and the horn of my salvation, and my high tower". The Alpha and Omega – He is Worthy to be Praised – Just bless Him anyhow…

2.  Thank Him for the past days. God has shown himself faithful. He deserves all the Praises, honor and adoration. Psalm 34:1-3, "I will bless the LORD at all times, His Praise shall continually be in my mouth…O magnify the LORD with me and let us exalt His name together."

3.  Father, fill my cup with provision. Let my cup run over, in Jesus' Name.

4.  Father, in this day of Joy, give me victory over the battles of the mind that have come to miniaturize my potentials, in Jesus' Name.

5.  Father, in any case I have come under the attack of spiritual forces of darkness in heavenly places against my joy, let the blood of Jesus fight for me and bring me victory in Jesus' Name. Father, let the carpenters of heaven scatter and destroy them, in Jesus' Name.

6.  Father, keep me from straying out of Your Presence, in Jesus' name.

7.  Thank you, LORD, for prayers answered. I receive full scale of joy now, in Jesus' name.

# DAY 29

# SONGS OF VICTORY

*"Then sang Moses and the children of Israel this song unto the LORD, and spake, saying, I will sing unto the LORD, for He hath triumphed gloriously: the horse and his rider hath He thrown into the sea. The LORD is my strength and song, and He is become my salvation: He is my God, and I will prepare Him an habitation; my father's God, and I will exalt Him" (Exodus 15:1-2) KJV.*

*"For, behold, I have made thee this day a defenced city, and an iron pillar, and brasen walls against the whole land, against the kings of Judah, against the princes thereof, against the priests thereof, and against the people of the land. And they shall fight against thee; but they shall not prevail against thee; for I am with thee, saith the LORD, to deliver thee" (Jeremiah 1:18-19) KJV*

I congratulate you for it is your day of "Songs of Victory". A day of celebration, the manifestation of the sons of God, divine lifting, harvest where you have not labored, crowning all your efforts with resounding success. It is the day when you'll begin to inherit houses you didn't build, vineyards you didn't plant, the church of Christ will be manifested, all the enemies of Israel shall be vanquished, and all drumbeats of intifada silenced forever! Please congratulate yourself because, finally, your light is breaking forth. I'm excited already and as the LORD lives, your testimony is guaranteed today, in Jesus' Name!

There is a heavenly artillery with invisible missiles that can be launched against every battle, opposition and confrontation that stands in your way today. There is a guaranteed provision for your dominion, a more-than-conqueror status in the conflicts of life. This is the platform for your prayers grounded in victory in every warfare of today.

God promised in His Word to be in you (1 John 4:4), for you (Romans 8:31), and with you (Jeremiah 1:19; Isaiah 43:2). That guarantees your unchallengeable, unstoppable, irresistible existence and stance in life's journey. When these portions of scripture become a revelation to you, and you build up your mind and attitude with them, every opposition will bow to you (Zechariah 4:6). You can command divine help (Psalms 121:1,2; Isaiah 50:7), and the LORD will begin to fight your battles (Exodus 14:14; Deuteronomy 20:1-4). Then, the LORD goes ahead of all your endeavors (Isaiah 45:1-31) commanding divine visitations (Jeremiah 29:10-14). At that point, you can establish your divinely attributed royalty status on earth (Romans 5:17; Revelations 1:5, 6).

We are created for responsibility. One very crucial responsibility we have is to contend for what God has given us (Deuteronomy 2:24). In the school of victory in life, possession is impossible without contention. What you don't contend for, you are not qualified for. Life is not a game of chance, accident, trial and error; it is a game of contention. God has guaranteed victory this season, but we need to contend for it before we can possess it. It is your visa into the city of your possession to enjoy the accomplishments of Calvary.

## What Must We Do in This New Day?

1. **Renewed Mind** - (Mentality of a Champion) Life battles are spiritual but fought in the mind. The ministry of God's Word is to renew and transform the mind (Romans 12:1-2). Constant meditation, inspiration and revelation of God's Word purges our minds from negative limitations and impossibilities, transforming us to a divine mindset (1 Corinthians 2:16). As you renew and fortify your mind by adequate deposits from God's Word, you remain stronger than your life's challenges. Confront life and your oppositions with this mentality and you will remain an ever-increasing winner and a champion in life's journey.

2. **Manifestation:** In Romans 8:18-25, "the creation waits in eager expectation for the sons of God to be revealed." Everything created – water system, education system, family system, banking system, etc. is waiting for us to be uncovered; to step out and be manifested. We need godly people showing up to lead, run, and manage them to glorify God. These worldly systems are moaning and groaning, waiting for us to show up, to manifest! As we sing the songs of victory, the real authentic you as designed by God shall show up and manifest God's purpose for us here on earth as Christ's ambassadors (2 Corinthians 5:20).

3. **Witnessing:** Before the LORD Jesus Christ returns, there will be evidence that God's kingdom exists. There will be a colony of people who will be the evidence of how good God is in bad times. These people will be a different culture on the earth that shows that heaven is present, demonstrating the goodness of God as they sing the songs of victory. They will be healthy people in times of sickness. They will be prosperous people in times of economic crises. They will have peace in times of turmoil. They will have lasting marriages filled with love in times of high divorce rates. This is the kingdom of God on earth (Matthew 6:9-13).

4. **Watchfulness:** Champions and winners are always watchful. They constantly question attitudes and habits that threaten their victory i.e. overeating, lack of exercise, and lack of knowledge. Matthew 26:41 says, "Watch and pray;" Psalms 37:34 says, "Wait on the LORD, and keep his way." Psalms 40:1 says, "I waited patiently for the LORD; and he inclined unto me, and heard my cry."

Let's examine a few things we can do to ensure that threats do not overtake us:

• Rise early and start the day off right: Spend time in the morning by yourself preparing your attitude for the day. As a leader/victor, you need to understand that your mood affects the mood of everyone around you.

• Always do the right thing: Everyone is constantly faced with integrity issues. Perhaps adding a little more to your expense report or telling a small lie can make things a little easier. But a small fire can soon lead to a catastrophe.

- Watch and pray: One well-known preacher says that every day he reads the Bible and the newspaper because he wants to know what both sides are doing. You need to have your finger on the pulse of your neighborhood, community, nation, and world. Isaiah 40:31 says, "But they that wait upon the LORD shall renew their strength; they shall mount up with wings as eagles; they shall run, and not be weary; and they shall walk, and not faint."

5. **Prayerfulness:** It is on our knees that the spiritual abortion of dreams is resisted; it is there that all miscarriage of visions are appropriately dealt with (James 5:16). There is no birth without pain. There is no delivery without labor (Isaiah 66:8). Desperate situations require desperate measures. The tragedy of our day is not unanswered prayers, but unoffered prayers. The man that will find God is the man who will seek Him (Isaiah 55:6). God is not found where he is not sought. He reveals Himself to the longing soul (Jeremiah 29:11). Travailing means labor, diligence, hard work, faithfulness, endurance, dedication, determination, consistency, and the like.

Welcome yourself into your day of dominion, distinction, triumphant lifestyle and from henceforth, you will never fail nor fall again, in Jesus' mighty Name!

# PRAYERS

1. Thank God for today. Thank Him for every area of your life and for seeing you through all the past days.

2. Thank Him for you are entering the new reality of the harvests of prayers answered, divine manifestations, season of gathering spoils in all areas of your life, and songs of victory as from today.

3. Pray for the Grace to carry the manifest Presence of God throughout your lifetime. I declare that God is with me and for me, in Jesus' Name.

4. From henceforth, I shall encounter no failure, no defeat and no disappointment until Christ returns, in Jesus' Name. I receive the anointing and empowerment for victory, in Jesus' Name!

5. Father, just as Saul got tired of pursuing after the life of David and slept off, put divine tiredness on all that pursue after my glory in life. Let them go into sleep, in Jesus' Name. Every opposition and confrontation organized along my pathways, scatter by fire, in Jesus' Name.

6. Father, give me a new song of victory to sing this day. I shall experience a prosperous, productive, and fulfilling day, in Jesus' Name.

7. Worship God with songs and thanksgiving. Your battle is won. Your victory is delivered. Begin to gather your spoils, in Jesus' mighty Name!

# DAY 30

# HALLELUJAH

*"...Then a voice came from the throne, saying, "Praise our God, all you His servants and those who fear Him, both small and great!" And I heard, as it were, the voice of a great multitude, as the sound of many waters and as the sound of mighty thunderings, saying, "Alleluia! For the LORD God Omnipotent reigns"* (Revelation 19:5-6).

We bless God for another new day. The theme yesterday was "Songs of Victory" and we prayed accordingly. Testimonies have been coming in about the acts of God in the life of men as His people begin to possess their possessions. Today, the LORD said it is our day of shouting Hallelujah. Hallelujah means 'God be praised'. It is an expression of rejoicing and of worship. As we shout Hallelujah to our LORD and King today, expect the unexpected, spiritually, emotionally, maritally, physically, etc. From one generation to the other, there is a common denominator in the lives of those who are truly great. It is that they all place premium value on giving

God His place in their lives through praise, worship and thanksgiving. The Psalmist recognized this when he said, "Let everything that hath breath praise the LORD. Praise ye the LORD" (Psalms 150:6).

When we come before God, there are two crucial people in the meeting - God and you. In that meeting, only one thing can be preeminent – your need or God. What you focus on becomes magnified. If you focus on your problem, it becomes overwhelming in your perception. But if you focus on the LORD Jesus Christ and praise Him, He will be magnified and your problems will fade to insignificance. "We have in our churches a great deal of prayer, but I think it would be a good thing if we had a praise meeting occasionally. If we could only get people to praise God for what He has done, it would be a good deal better than asking Him continually for something" (D.L. Moody).

Here are some significant things you can receive this day by singing Hallelujah to the LORD:

- Enjoyment of His Divine Presence - Psalms 22:3, 114:4-9.

- Hearing from God more clearly - Psalms 29:1-3.

- Experiencing the wonder working power of God - Acts 16:25-26.

- Increase in the attraction of favor - Acts 2:47; Mark 6:21-23.

- Witnessing supernatural breakthroughs - 2 Chronicles 20:17-22.

- Satisfaction of fresh anointing daily - Psalms 92:1-2,10.

- Provoking the presence of the Holy Spirit – 1 Samuel 16:13.

- Assurance of an unbroken fellowship with the Holy Spirit.

- Beginning to do the impossible, hear the inaudible, and see the invisible – Isaiah 54:1-3; 2 Kings 3:15-17

- Acceleration of the manifestation of expected miracles - Habakkuk 3:17-19.

It is well established that the LORD of LORDs inhabits the praises of His people (Psalms 22:3). When you live a life full of praise to God, His Presence abides with you. When He abides with you, He compels signs and miracles to attend to you. In Psalms 112, when the children of Israel came out of Egypt, God was their sanctuary. The sea saw them and fled. Likewise, Jordan was driven back, and the mountains skipped like rams; the little hills like young lambs. It was God's Presence that took them through the Red Sea and gave them victory over their enemies.

For the rest of today, we just want to appreciate Him, thank Him, honor Him, adore Him, dance before Him and sing praises unto Him. Even if you were about to be executed like Paul and Silas in Acts 16, because of the Hallelujah connection, the miraculous will happen. There will be an earthquake and your prison gates shall fling open and your chains fall off in Jesus' Name. In 2 Chronicles 20:17, the Scriptures say, "Ye shall not need to fight in this battle: set yourselves, stand ye still, and see the salvation of the LORD with you, O Judah and Jerusalem: fear not, nor be dismayed; tomorrow go out against them [in Praises!]: for the LORD will be with you." (Emphasis mine).

Many years ago, there was no rainfall in one of the cities in America. This led to a drought and poor harvests. The farmers gathered to pray. They prayed for days and nothing happened. Then one day, one of them suggested that they should begin to shout Hallelujah, sing praises and thank God for rain; "...calling those things which be not as though they were" (Romans 4:17). The praises moved heaven and not long after, rain came in torrents. They sang their way from famine to fruitfulness. Make God your priority this day [and always] and He will make you His priority.

## PRAYERS

1. Father, I have reasons to praise you and I begin to sing my reasons unto you now, in Jesus' Name. My pregnancy was not aborted, and presently I am still alive and in the right frame of mind. The restoration, favor, health, family, love and change of status that I have received.

2. Isaiah 52:9 says, "Break forth into joy, sing together, ye waste places of Jerusalem: for the LORD hath comforted his people, he hath redeemed Jerusalem." Sing of His mercies forever.

3. I command every sorrow of my heart to give way to songs of praise unto my God now, in Jesus' Name. Father, send me helpers of Joy, in Jesus' Name.

4. I relocate from the camp of the murmurers and grumblers, in Jesus' Name (1 Corinthians 10:10).

5. Every agenda of sorrow and tragedy drawn up by my enemy is destroyed and shall neither stand, nor come to pass, in Jesus' Name.

6. I declare loud and clear that the joy of the LORD is

my strength.

7.  As the LORD liveth and my soul liveth, no one in my
    family will shed tears of sorrow this year and in the
    years to come, in Jesus' Name.

8.  O LORD, I have sown in tears long enough, let me
    begin to reap JOY from now on, in Jesus' Name
    (Psalms 126:1-6).

9.  Let everything that hath breath praise the LORD –
    Praise the LORD!

## HYMN - A NEW THING

(Written and composed by Pastor E.A. Adeboye,
General Overseer of RCCG Worldwide)

1. We will soon shout Halleluyah
Because GOD will do new things
Sinners will soon be forgiven
Prodigals will come home soon.

Chorus:
*Shout Halleluyah*
*Because God will do new things*
*Rivers in desert now flowing*
*Halleluyah to our king*

2. We will soon shout Halleluyah
Because God will do new things
Sickness and sorrow will be gone
Bondage will be forgotten.

3. We will soon shout Halleluyah
Because God will do new things
The barren will be fruitful soon
Failure will be forgotten

4. We will soon shout Halleluyah
Because God will do new things
Poverty will be forgotten
Stagnancy will soon be gone.

5. We will soon shout Hallelujah
Because God will do new things
To all miracles are given
There shall be celebrations

6. We will soon shout Halleluyah
Because God will do new things
Many will have testimonies
Of prayers answered fully

7. We will soon shout Hallcluyah
Because God will do new things
One of us will chase a thousand
Two will conquer ten thousand.

8. We will soon shout Halleluyah
Because God will do new things
Songs of praises we will sing
Halleluyah to our King

# DAY 31

# AMEN

*"... For all the promises of God in Him are Yes, and in Him Amen, to the glory of God through us...";* *"... And to the angel of the church of the Laodiceans write, 'These things says the Amen, the Faithful and True Witness, the Beginning of the creation of God"* *(2 Corinthians 1:20; Revelation 3:14).*

I bring you glad tidings in this beautiful day that the LORD has made. We've enjoyed various blessings of God through amazing themes and prophetic words. Today, we are commanded to shout a resounding and powerful AMEN! That's His Word for us this day; "AMEN."

## WHAT IS AMEN?

God would rather not speak, than say what He will not do. He always ensures that His Word does not return to Him empty. Unlike Man, there is no promise too hard for God to fulfill. The passage of time never invalidates His Promise. "So, shall My Word be that goeth forth out of My mouth: it shall not return unto Me void, but it shall accomplish that which

I please, and it shall prosper in the thing whereto I sent it" (Isaiah 55:11). Every word of prophecy from the beginning until now will surely happen, in the Name of Jesus. The Hebrew word 'amen' means "true and binding; truly; that which is sure and valid, confirmed, supported, or upheld" (American Heritage Dictionary). Thus, when Jesus begins certain sayings by declaring "Amen, amen, I say to you . ." or rendered "truly, truly" or "verily, verily," one might also translate it "certainly, certainly" or "most assuredly" (Evangelical Dictionary of Theology).

## JESUS IS THE AMEN

From both Revelation 3:14 and 2 Corinthians 1:20 quoted above, Jesus is the Amen! He is the Faithful and True Witness. He is ever faithful, ever sure! Numbers 23:19 assures us that, "God is not a man, that He should lie; neither the son of man, that He should repent: hath He said, and shall He not do it? Or hath He spoken, and shall He not make it good?" In addition, Colossians 2:9-10 says, "For in Him dwelleth all the fullness of the Godhead bodily. And ye are complete in Him, which is the Head of all principality and power."

## AMEN – A UNIVERSAL LANGUAGE

If you get the chance to, you can listen to a person pray in Chinese or Japanese or Swahili or German or French or Russian or Arabic, and very likely there is at least one word you will understand: "Amen." It would probably be pronounced differently, but it ought to still be discernible.

So, what we have all over the world today is a word, "Amen," that is a direct transliteration from the Hebrew language.

Therefore, when one says, "amen" in response to a prayer, it serves as an affirmation of agreement with the content of the prayer; an expression of faith that God will hear and act favorably on the prayer. Paul spoke to the church in Corinth, and while teaching on the word "Amen" said, "If you pray so people can't understand you, how will they say "Amen" (1 Corinthians 14:16)? Therefore, when a man or woman of God pours out his heart to God in a circle of prayer, the right response should be a deeply felt "Amen" in unison. It is also important to note that in the Old Testament the word "amen" was mainly a congregational response to give a strong affirmation or agreement to a curse or a word of blessing from God (Elwell, 1997).

## PEOPLE THAT EXPERIENCED THE "AMEN" OF GOD

- In the deliverance of the children of Israel, God promised that He would set them free from captivity after 400 years. Their salvation did not come any sooner because they never cried and asked for deliverance; they seemed to have settled for living in misery. However, when they cried, God delivered them. God always ensures that His promises happen. This case of the children of Israel is a confirmation of Him keeping His promise, regardless of the passage of time prior to fulfillment. I pray for you today that every one of God's promises to you shall be fulfilled in your life, in Jesus' Name.

- There is no prayer too hard for God to answer. As believers, we occasionally ask God for things that seem difficult for Him to deliver. Elijah told Elisha that his request for a double portion of Elijah's spirit was almost impossible (2 Kings 2:9-10). However, the ever faithful, ever-sure Amen came through and Elisha did twice as many miracles as his spiritual father.

- At times, one is in a dire situation and it appears God is running late, as was the case with Lazarus (John 11:1-44). Jesus brought Lazarus back to life after he had been dead and buried for four days. I pray for you again that every seemingly hard or delayed situation in your life shall meet with God's Resolution today, in Jesus' Name.

- In Genesis 32:24-33:11, Jacob had the encounter of a lifetime that resulted in a divine blessing and a change of name. That blessing caused a change of heart in his previously estranged twin brother, who had sworn to kill him the next time they both saw each other.

- Blind Bartimaeus received a new lease on life when the LORD Jesus attended to him, despite the adversaries all around trying to shout him down. His cry for help was, "Jesus (Amen), Jesus (Amen)...Son of David, have mercy on me" (Mark 10:47-49). (Emphasis mine).

We all experience difficult situations in our lives, regardless of our experiences, spirituality or knowledge. Abraham, Job, Moses, Paul, John are all patriarchs of faith, yet they faced difficult situations. However, the Amen, ever faithful, ever sure came through for them. God loves to take the lost, the last, the least, and the lowest to make something beautiful out of their lives that He may gain maximal glory. He is inviting you to come to Him that you might be made whole. The Holy Bible is replete with stories of people who walked the face of this earth, long before our ancestors, and experienced the Amen of God with the result of the impossible made possible. I declare that it is your turn, your time, your season to experience the AMEN of God. As the LORD lives, you will not enter the next day without a shout of Amen! Halleluyah! in Jesus' Name (Psalms 65:11).

# PRAYERS

1. Father, thank You; Promise Keeper, Miracle Worker, Light in the Darkness, Monarch of the Universe, The Unchanging Changer, thank You.

2. Every standing covenant with the devil that is giving the devil a legal access into my life, be revoked and annulled right now by fire, in Jesus' Name

3. Father, hasten to deliver me from every problem that is mocking you in my life.

4. Wisdom to understand the times, seasons and purposes of God for my life, come upon me as from today, in Jesus' Name.

5. Father, please reverse the irreversible in my life and let every of your promises to me come to fulfillment, in Jesus' Name.

6. I receive power for expansion and enlargement, breaking through and breaking forth on all areas of my life as from today, in Jesus' Name.

7. Crown this day for me with your goodness. Psalms 65:11 says, "You have crowned the year with Your bounty, and Your paths drip with fatness."